A. J. Cronin

Twayne's English Authors Series

Kinley E. Roby, Editor

Northeastern University

TEAS 398

A. J. CRONIN
(1896–1981)
Photograph courtesy of
Victor Gollancz, Ltd.

A. J. Cronin

By Dale Salwak

Citrus College

Twayne Publishers • Boston

A. J. Cronin

Dale Salwak

Copyright © 1985 by G. K. Hall & Company
All Rights Reserved
Published by Twayne Publishers
A Division of G. K. Hall & Co.
A publishing subsidiary of ITT
70 Lincoln Street
Boston, Massachusetts 02111

Book Production by Lyda E. Kuth
Book Design by Barbara Anderson

Printed on permanent/durable acid-free
paper and bound in the United States of
America.

Library of Congress Cataloging in Publication Data

Salwak, Dale.
    A. J. Cronin.

    (Twayne's English authors series ; TEAS 398)
    Bibliography: p. 145
    Includes index.
    1. Cronin, A. J. (Archibald Joseph), 1896– —
Criticism and interpretation.   I. Title.   II. Series.
PR6005.R68Z88   1985   823'.912   83-25304
ISBN 0-8057-6884-X

For
Martie Dunham

Contents

About the Author

Dale Salwak graduated with honors from Purdue University (1969) and received his M.A. (1970) and Ph.D. (1974) degrees in English Literature from the University of Southern California under a National Defense Education Act competitive fellowship program. As a faculty member of Southern California's Citrus College since 1973, Professor Salwak specializes in contemporary English and American literature, advanced composition, and the Bible as literature. He is also the author of *Kingsley Amis: A Reference Guide* (1978), *John Braine and John Wain: A Reference Guide* (1980), *John Wain* (1981), and *A. J. Cronin: A Reference Guide* (1982), all published by G. K. Hall & Co., and of a collection of interviews he conducted with Kingsley Amis, John Braine, John Wain, and Colin Wilson entitled *Literary Voices* (Borgo Press, 1984). His forthcoming books include a critical study of Kingsley Amis and a collection of essays on Barbara Pym.

Preface

Hatter's Castle (1931), *The Stars Look Down* (1935), *The Citadel* (1937), and *The Keys of the Kingdom* (1941) established A. J. Cronin as one of the English-speaking world's most prominent and popular authors of his time. Everything that he wrote was stamped by his personality, his sincerity, his direct concern with ethical issues, his seemingly instinctive knowledge of ordinary people, and his extraordinary gift for storytelling. Sixteen novels, a play, an autobiography, and one of the most highly praised British television series ever made represent a career that spans one-half of the twentieth century—1930 to 1978—and of a life that was itself as engrossing and multifaceted as his fiction.

And yet, although many of his novels have sold in the millions and have been handsomely adapted to the motion picture screen, they are a topic "strangely neglected" by academic criticism. The best essay on his work remains Francis Fytton's "Dr. Cronin: An Essay in Victoriana," published as long ago as 1956. There have been other essays, before and since, and there are several perceptive pages in John T. Frederick's "A. J. Cronin" (*College English,* 1941) and in Daniel Horton Davies's book, *A Mirror of the Ministry in Modern Novels* (1959). There remain to be studied, however, the rapport between Cronin and his readers; the relationship between his life and works; his devotion to Catholicism and social justice; and the historical interest of his novels, their nineteenth-century parallels, sources, and influences. Altogether, the aim of this book is to urge its readers to a fresh reading of the original. The cumulative effect of Cronin's work over the last fifty-five years has been a striking one, and my intention is to capture that effect, to bring it together between the covers of a single book.

I have chosen a strategy that is simple and direct: first a discussion of the background details useful to an understanding of his works; then a close reading of all of his novels in their order of publication; and finally an assessment of his career at a time when his writings are generating a new and heartening resurgence both in America and abroad.

A study such as this can never be considered an individual effort. It is a pleasure to express my gratitude to others who have played so important a role in its completion. I owe a great debt to Vincent Cronin, his son, and Michael Blaber, his editor at Little, Brown, both of whom read the entire manuscript and offered valuable suggestions for its improvement; however, any shortcomings in the published work should be attributed entirely to me.

For their kind assistance in gathering materials, I should also like to thank the research assistants at the University of London Library, the University of Southern California Doheny Memorial Library, the Huntington Library, the University of California at Los Angeles Research Library, and the Library of Congress. For their diligent help and encouragement I should mention especially Mrs. Dorothy M. Brandt, New York, and Professors Bernard Zavidowsky and Eugene A. Taylor, Jr., Citrus College.

Finally, my deepest gratitude must go once again to my mother, Frances H. Salwak, who skillfully checked and corrected all drafts of the typescript, helped to proofread the galleys and page proofs, and assisted with the task of compiling the index; to my father, Stanley F. Salwak, President Emeritus, University of Maine at Presque Isle, whose keen interest in Cronin awakened my own and helped me to question the neglect into which he had fallen; and to my wife, Patricia—the most important person throughout the long gestation period of the book.

Dale Salwak

Citrus College

Chronology

1896   Archibald Joseph Cronin born 19 July in Cardross (Dumbartonshire), Scotland, to Patrick and Jessie Cronin.

1903   Father dies.

1908–1914   Attends Dumbarton Academy.

1914–1919   Educated at Glasgow University.

1916–1918   Serves in the European War as a surgeon sublieutenant.

1918   Works at the Locklea Asylum.

1919   Graduates Glasgow University, M.B., Ch.B. (honors).

1919–1921   Practices medicine, South Wales and London; physician to outpatients, Bellahouston Ministry of Pension Hospital.

1921   Medical Officer, Northumberland.

1921–1924   General Practice, London.

1921   Marries Agnes Mary Gibson.

1923   Glasgow University, D.Ph.

1924   Glasgow University, M.R.C.P. (Member of the Royal College of Physicians).

1924–1925   Medical Inspector of Mines for Great Britain, South Wales.

1925   *A History of Aneurism* (M.D. thesis).

1926   *Report on Dust Inhalation in Haematite Mines.*

1927   *Investigations in First-Aid Organization at Collieries in Great Britain.*

1930   Leaves medicine to pursue a writing career.

1931   *Hatter's Castle.*

1932   *Three Loves.*

1933   *Grand Canary.*

1935   *The Stars Look Down.*

1936   *Kaleidoscope in K.*

1937   *The Citadel;* Honorary D.Litt., Bowdoin College.

1939   Moves his family to Maine.

1940   *Jupiter Laughs.*

1941–1945   Works for the British Ministry of Information in the United States.

1941   *The Keys of the Kingdom.*

1942   Film version of *The Keys of the Kingdom.*

1944   *The Green Years.*

1948   *Shannon's Way;* moves his family to Connecticut.

1950   *The Spanish Gardener.*

1952   *Adventures in Two Worlds.*

1953   *Beyond This Place.*

1954   D.Litt, Lafayette College, Easton, Pennsylvania.

1955   Changes domicile to Switzerland.

1956   *A Thing of Beauty.*

1958   *The Northern Light;* "The Innkeeper's Wife."

1961   *The Judas Tree.*

1962   Mother dies.

1964   *A Song of Sixpence.*

1968   Wife enters Canadian nursing home.

1969   *A Pocketful of Rye; Adventures of a Black Bag.*

1975   *Desmonde.*

1978   *Doctor Finlay of Tannochbrae.*

1981   Dies 6 January in Valmont Clinic, at Glion (near Territet) in the Swiss canton of Vaud; buried 9 January at La Tour de Peilz.

Chapter One

The Two Worlds of A. J. Cronin

In the spring of 1930 a tall, sandy-haired, genial physician sold his London practice and home, moved with his family to an isolated farmhouse near Inverary, Scotland, and at the age of thirty-four wrote a novel for the first time in his life. *Hatter's Castle,* published the following year by Victor Gollancz, became an immediate success. It was the first novel to be chosen by the English Book Society for the book-of-the-month. It was later translated into many languages, dramatized, and made into a Paramount motion picture starring James Mason and Deborah Kerr. Before long, critics hailed A. J. Cronin as a new and important author, whose writing was comparable in content and style to that of Charles Dickens, Thomas Hardy, and Honoré de Balzac.

Cronin and his wife moved to a small apartment in London and then on to a modest cottage in Sussex, where he went to work on another novel, *Three Loves.* His popularity continued to increase following *Grand Canary* and *The Stars Look Down;* and helped greatly by an avid public in the United States, the ex-physician became something of a literary lion, in demand at dinners, bazaars, and book fairs. His writing launched him upon a literary career with such impetus that, once and for all, he "hung up [his] stethoscope and put away that little black bag—[his] medical days were over."[1]

The physician-novelist is of course by no means an unfamiliar literary figure. Arthur Conan Doyle, before he became immortal as the creator of Sherlock Holmes, wrote a book of short stories, *Around the Red Lamp* (1879), about his medical experiences. W. Somerset Maugham's first novel, *Liza of Lambeth* (1897), was the direct outcome of his experiences as a medical student and his work in hospitals. C. S. Forster studied medicine before

he dipped into the Napoleonic wars and brought Horatio Horn-
blower to port. Oliver Goldsmith, John Keats, Oliver Wendell
Holmes, William Carlos Williams, Sir Thomas Browne, and
the poet laureate of England, Robert Bridges, also had rich
medical backgrounds into which they reached for their books.
None of these examples, however, can quite parallel the dual
career of Cronin. Medicine with him was not a stopgap or step-
ping-stone. He was an outstanding financial and professional
success; moreover, he was ambitious, desperately tenacious, and
single-minded in his pursuit of that success. It was hard won
and well deserved. His second success, in an entirely different
field, was equally substantial. Although his popularity has suffered the temporary wane usual in the years immediately after
an author's death, Cronin was for long one of the best-known
and most controversial of British writers; through a number
of books remarkable for their honesty and realism, he helped
entertain and educate a generation of readers. As a writer, he
was always promoting tolerance, integrity, and social justice.
His favorite theme was that man should learn to be creative
rather than acquisitive, altruistic rather than selfish.

Before Cronin's books can be appreciatively read, we must
have a reasonable acquaintance with his life. This is not necessar-
ily true in the case of many writers, whose private lives are
less clearly reflected in their work than are those of such writers
as Dickens and Maugham, to whom Cronin bears a resemblance
in this matter. Throughout his career as a novelist, Cronin drew
heavily on his memories of what he had actually observed.
Henry James's argument that the writer of fiction should be
"one upon whom nothing is lost" received an emphatic embodiment in the life of Cronin, whose experiences as a child, a
medical student, and a physician are woven inextricably into
the fabric of his novels.

The Child (1896–1914)

Like so many of his fictional characters, young Archibald Joseph Cronin led a life that was by no means idyllic. As it is
recorded in his autobiography, *Adventures in Two Worlds* (1952),
his life had strong elements of the Cinderella story, though in
Cronin's case the period of trial was long. He was born in

Cardross (Dumbartonshire), Scotland, on 19 July 1896, the only child of a middle-class family whose fortunes were soon to decline rapidly. His mother, Jessie Montgomerie, was a Scottish Protestant woman who had defied her family—and a host of ancestors—by marrying an Irishman and turning Catholic. His father, Patrick Cronin, was a mercantile agent who until his death was able to offer his family a fairly comfortable existence. After the death of his father seven years later, however, young Cronin was forced to retreat with his penniless mother to the bitter and poverty-stricken home of her parents. The next ten years were to be a period of "unbelievable hardship" (6).

To most neighbors and relatives in the small, strictly moral and sternly Protestant town of Cardross, Jessie Montgomerie's marriage and conversion were considered a disgrace, and upon her son they inflicted the inevitable ridicule and persecution. On the one hand, there was sectarian antagonism, not far short of that which has erupted in recent years in Northern Ireland as violence. On the other hand, there was the stern Protestant morality. "I was afraid in the strict tradition that if I did wrong I should be punished for it," Cronin wrote. "That was called justice."[2] One experience in particular typifies how the boy was made to feel humiliatingly disoriented and alien to his new environment:

He was very, very poor, and one morning his grandfather lined the whole family up to select one of them as a companion for a trip to the Clyde. "Joe" was chosen. He was so excited with the preliminaries of the trip and thought of the lovely boat ride, that when his grandfather put a huge meal before him, he couldn't eat a bite. Grandfather became furious and scolded the little boy soundly, but at that the nerves in his throat became all the tighter. "What a lad, what a lad," said Grandfather. "I wish I had taken one of the others. Wastin' good food ye are lik that." He never heard the end of it.[3]

During those early years Cronin's first responsibility was not to be troublesome. If he could accomplish that, he felt he could move along to his second responsibility: to make himself loved in a strange home and strange town. But it was not easy. He was a Catholic, and these people were not. His clothes proclaimed him an alien, and so did his speech. Cronin was marked permanently by an environment that was noisy, quarrelsome, profoundly unhappy, and emotionally dramatic—a source of endless material for the future novelist.

Cronin's delight in reading and learning perhaps compensated for his frustrations. Among the authors he read were Robert Louis Stevenson (an only child like himself and a firm favorite right to the end of his life), Sir Walter Scott, Guy de Maupassant, Charles Dickens, W. Somerset Maugham, and Samuel Butler— whose *The Way of All Flesh* (1903) Cronin cited as his favorite book. (Cronin even began his writing career as a conscious "disciple" of Butler.) At Cardross Village School and later at Dumbarton Academy, where literature was his best subject, the boy became something of a prodigy, repeatedly winning prizes and discovering in himself that love for learning that would be a source of stability all his life. He was often engaged, he remembered, in the "reprehensible habit of winning medals for essays."[4] At thirteen he won the Gold Medal in a nationwide contest for best historical essay. Both as a student and, later in life, as a physician-writer, he spent enormous stretches of time at his desk, wrestling with his work. This compulsiveness, combined with his intelligence and his eagerness, won Cronin the approbation of both his uncle—a canon of the Catholic Church, who used part of his private means to pay for his nephew's schooling and later became the model for Father Chisholm in *The Keys of the Kingdom*—and his great-grandfather, who later became the model for Alexander Gow in *The Green Years.*

Yet Cronin's talent also meant he would suffer the emotions of premature loneliness that so often afflict an unusually bright boy. He was highly regarded by his teachers, but other students—and their parents—sometimes resented his abilities. One father, whose young hopeful son was beaten by Cronin in an important examination, became so enraged that years later *Hatter's Castle* took shape around his domineering personality.[5] The theme—"the tragic record of a man's egotism and bitter pride" (261)—suggests the dark and often melodramatic atmosphere of Cronin's early novels. In them, some characters are drawn with humorous realism, but for the most part humor is dimmed by gloomy memories of his own neglected childhood, and sensational scenes are shrouded in an atmosphere genuinely eerie and sinister. Inevitably, Cronin clung to the notion that between

the life of the mind and the life of the senses, between a disciplined commitment to scholarship and a need to share in the
common pleasures of mankind, there is an irremediable conflict.
The religious bigotry, the family's unceasing poverty, the interest in learning—this trio of forces worked at shaping the
young Cronin. A shy, sensitive, lonely boy, aware of his peculiarities yet hungry for the townspeople's acceptance, he developed,
like Robert Shannon of *The Green Years,* an overt mistrust for
organized religion. Until his father's death, Cronin had been
devout, and the question of his becoming a clergyman may
have been considered; but if he had entertained such ambitions,
his increasing indifference, which emerges clearly in his novels,
must have caused him to abandon such plans.

In spite of the religious conflicts and the later intellectual
skepticism of his medical days, Cronin remained a spiritually
sensitive person. An underlying, even when unrecognized, belief in man's spiritual integrity continued to be a major motivat-
ing influence in his own life. In his maturity, after he returned
to the Church, he was to have an almost inordinate affection
for the underdog, and he most deeply sympathized with those
who suffered from any form of intolerance. In 1952 he would
write:

When a man surveys his past from middle age he must surely ask
himself what those bygone years have taught him. If I have learned
anything in the swift unrolling of the web of time . . . it is the virtue
of tolerance, of moderation in thought and deed, of forbearance toward
one's fellow men. These were qualities sadly lacking in my furious
youth. (328)

When we consider the various elements in Cronin's unhappy
childhood, it is not surprising to find that the lure of "riches,
high position, fame" (7) dominated his thoughts. He has asserted that his relationship with those who raised him was vital
in determining the course of his career: "Nothing can exceed
the longing of a poor youth, beaten down by circumstances,
to rise above misfortune and justify himself, not only in his
own eyes but in the eyes of others" (7). Out of this longing
there developed the faith that he could succeed if only he worked
hard enough, used his wits, and became self-reliant. With an

impulsiveness and dogged determination that was also to be a
hallmark of his heroes, he decided to earn enough money from
menial jobs to become a doctor.

He chose this career, he said, because it was the only thing
for an ambitious boy living in Scotland to do. "The Scottish
view is very practical. You can have medicine or you can have
divinity! I chose the lesser evil."[6] According to his later view,
however, what he wanted to be was a writer; but "naturally if
I'd told them that back home in Scotland, they'd have thought
I was wrong in the head. I had to do something sensible, instead.
That's why I went in for medicine. It was safe and practical."[7]
When, having just turned eighteen, he entered Glasgow University, the next chapter of his life opened to him. There for the
first time he would be entirely on his own.

The Medical Student (1914–21)

Cronin had begun his medical studies when World War I
took him into the Royal Navy Volunteer Reserve as a surgeon
sublieutenant. After he was demobilized in 1918, he returned
to the university with no money, no influential friends, only a
strong determination to "do anything and everything, to enable
me to take my doctor's degree" (4). Too often meals consisted
of a roll and a cup of weak tea. The only outfit he had to
wear was his old naval uniform. To buy his instruments and
used textbooks he had to pawn the gold watch and chain he
had inherited from his father. He must have been daunted, if
not discouraged, when one of his professors, the formidable
Dr. William McEwen, predicted: "In medicine, or some other
field, I believe that you may make your mark. But of one thing
I am sure. You will never be a surgeon" (12).

Nevertheless, Cronin persevered. To earn food and shelter
while he studied, he worked first as a clinical clerk at Locklea
Asylum for the Insane, one of the best institutions of its kind
in Scotland. Here he learned things about the human mind
that were to be useful many years later. For one hundred guineas
and board he was responsible for dispensing, examining specimens, and feeding patients. Open, eager, and imaginative, he
was also one of the greener, more gullible students. One experience could have ended his career: he was nearly strangled to

death by George Blair, a patient whom he had urged the superintendent to release as "such a decent chap" (18). This experience provided material for an important scene in *Three Loves,* wherein Lucy Moore is attacked by a female lunatic.

The side of his work that impressed him most deeply was that of attending the women of Dublin, whose slum dwellings lay close to the Rotunda Hospital, where he enrolled in a three-month course in obstetrics. Down those "ill-lit streets" and up those "dark stone stairs" of the high tenements went young Cronin, clutching his black doctor's bag (23). In company with a classmate, Hugh Devers, he spent many hours both day and night in "this dreadful environment" (23), attending to the women. During the obligatory postnatal care, Cronin visited his patients twice daily for a period of two weeks, to wash and change the babies. His attentive eyes took in every detail. At the same time, the experiences stimulated an interest in the problems of the poor that was to have such a lasting effect upon Cronin:

Gradually we lost our earlier exuberance, became attuned to a more sober mood. Indeed, it was here, in the slums of Dublin, that I became aware, for the first time, of the patience and endurance, the sublime fortitude of the very poor. Many moving instances of courage and self-sacrifice came to our notice, and . . . made a lasting impression upon me. (23)

Along with these experiences, Cronin was struck forcefully by the contrast between his sincere idealism and the cynicism, selfishness, and muddled incompetency of many of the students and doctors he met. This conflict later found expression in his fiction, in which his idealized heroes' enthusiasm is contrasted sharply with the satirical descriptions of other doctors, civic officials, and small-town bigots. In *The Stars Look Down, The Citadel, The Green Years,* and *Shannon's Way,* for example, many aspects of the medical profession are criticized: medical schools, small-town politics, public health, fashionable clinics, and even research centers. We may judge with what spirit Cronin left the university from the following judgment, written the year *The Citadel* appeared and on the occasion of being criticized by the British Medical Association for his apparent attack on the profession:

When, freshly hatched from my medical school I faced the world
with a chubby textbook confidence, I realized with real compunction
what a danger to society I must have been. My first essay with the
chloroform bottle nearly killed my patient. In my initial adventure
in obstetrics I nearly killed myself. My instrumental teaching, you
see, had entailed walking out once, before a ribald class, to apply
forceps upon a dilapidated wooden model. The reality, at 2 o'clock
of a murky Welsh morning in the sweating back bedroom of a miner's
house, was less hilarious.[8]

Having been graduated M.B., Ch.B. with honors in 1919,
Cronin continued his studies and training. During this period
he was impressed by three personalities who eventually made
their way into his novels. One individual was Hasan, an Indian
Serang whom he met in 1919 aboard the *S. S. Rawalpindar,*
an overcrowded liner bound from Liverpool to Calcutta. Cronin
had been hired as the temporary doctor, and Hasan was his
assistant. When a smallpox epidemic broke out, it was their
job to treat the cases and keep the news from the fifteen hundred
passengers. In Hasan, the young doctor was confronted with
virtues and qualities he admired: dependability, self-control,
faith, and, most important, a contempt for "all personal advantage" (37).

Also aboard the ship was a British couple who particularly
caught Cronin's attention. Cronin documented the voyage carefully and made detailed notes about this couple, later to be
used in *Grand Canary.* The lady had "a high, 'well-bred' voice"
(28). Her companion was "a young man with a military yet
foppish air" (28). Both carried their Britishness with them like
an ostentatious piece of baggage. They refused, as a matter
almost of conscience, to speak of Hasan as anything but "an
absurdly comic creature" (28). Thus Cronin's sense of the super-
ficiality and the cruelty of many people was enlarged by this
pettiness and this unbounded and unwarranted contempt for
the working poor. As his career progressed, Cronin found his
own passion for material success combined with a growing distrust of the pride of the spirit that comes with it. This concept
finds expression throughout his novels.

A second influential figure was "Dr. Cameron," an ailing
old Scot, a general practitioner living in "Tannochbrae,"[9] a

village in the West Highlands. As assistant to the stern, practical, hardworking doctor, later used as the prototype for Dr. Page in *The Citadel,* Cronin learned important lessons. Once he missed a toy in a child's nose and diagnosed the case as a lung ailment. This incident and others taught him about the problems of diagnosis. There is nothing "more supremely difficult," he wrote, "for here the temptation is to assess the existing symptoms simply on their face value" (71). Another time he lost all of his savings from investing in gold mine stocks on the advice of a patient. Learning of this, Dr. Cameron confronted him: "Let me tell you plainly you're not the man you were. You're changing . . . losing your sense of values. And more. You're doing rank bad work. I'm both disappointed and dissatisfied with it" (117). Once again Cronin had learned an important lesson about his passion for material success.

But it was Agnes Mary Gibson—known in her family as May— who was destined to play the most crucial role in his life. She was the daughter of the well-to-do owner of a bakery business, and socially his superior. They first met as fellow students at Glasgow University. Cronin found her immensely attractive, and under the stress of medical studies an instant friendship was formed. What struck the Gibsons about Cronin, apart from his good looks, was his sense of humor. Hard worker though he was, he could be counted on to see the funny side of most situations; he liked dressing up, mimicking, teasing. Little of this world would appear in his writing, and it became a joke between Cronin and May's younger sister Netta that one day he would write a book about her that would make her laugh, as he so often did in his medical student days.[10]

In many ways it was a friendship of opposites. Where Cronin was "happy-go-lucky and fiercely ambitious," May was "quiet, modest, and reserved" (5). Where she was a Protestant—and a devout one—he was a Catholic, and hardly devout. Their friends pointed out their "mutual unsuitability," and from time to time they "met in agonized confabulation, whereat, over more tea and buns, [they] palely pledged [them]selves to common sense, then parted, heroically, forever" (5). But no sooner had they done so than, next morning, they came together again and vowed that they "would never give each other up" (5)— an indication of both their idealism and their shared love.

In May Gibson the young medical student found a kindred spirit. Her enthusiasm, her love of walking and the open air, her experiences at the university—all seemed to echo Cronin's own interests and tastes. Like Cronin, too, she was an intelligent person of tremendous powers of memory (later she would help him by checking his manuscripts for errors). And so when May graduated from medical school, Cronin asked her to be his wife. May's father would never have allowed her to marry in a Catholic church. As it happened, Cronin's religious faith then burned low, and he felt no compunction about agreeing to wed in the church where the Gibsons regularly worshipped. In spite of the warnings of friends and relatives, they married and moved to the slag-strewn mining town in the Rhondda Valley, South Wales, where through the poverty and success she remained a faithful, loyal, and devoted companion, and where began the next phase of Cronin's life.

The Physician (1921–30)

"It has been said that the medical profession proves the best training ground for a novelist," Cronin wrote, "since there it is possible to see people with their masks off."[11] Certainly, in his own writings, Cronin drew heavily upon his experiences as a doctor. He spent nine formative years in the profession from 1921, when he practiced in a Welsh mining community, to 1930, when he was established as a well-to-do physician in London's West End. These years gave him the opportunity to observe a variety of characters. He also learned to look upon the harsh facts of life, upon pain, bereavement, and incurable disease with compassion, an attitude that found its way into his novels. And throughout these early experiences and contacts with people of every kind, he kept thinking, "what stories I could make out of them" (255). Though Cronin still expected to continue his work as a physician, his instincts were already those of a writer, and keeping a journal was intuitive preparation.

Adjusting to their new life in the Rhondda Valley was not easy for the young couple. May Cronin admitted that the day they arrived, after they had made their way through the ugly town and reached the furnished rooms in the miner's cottage that was to be their first home, she sat down and wept.[12] Cronin recalled how on his wedding night he left his bride to descend nine hundred feet into a coal mine, and there under a collapsing roof he amputated the leg of a trapped miner. Also, in this terrible town there was no hospital, no ambulance, no X-ray, and a great many diseases and accidents with which Cronin had to deal. He battled a scarlet fever epidemic and traced it to the farmer who was distributing the tainted milk. He pulled fishbones out of throats, delivered babies, and almost lost his nerve in a desperate struggle against diphtheria when he had to lance a child's throat without an anesthetic. Through all of these experiences Cronin was stockpiling memories that one day he would utilize fictionally.

Offered a better-paying job six months later at the neighboring valley of Tredegar, Cronin and his wife left Rhondda, an easy decision to make, and an essential one if he were to rise in the world. This too was a colliery town; but unlike the Rhondda Valley, "it was trim and clean and set on the verge of still unspoiled hill country" (160). This country allowed the Cronins to walk for hours at a time while thinking—sometimes brooding—but continually delighted by the natural spectacle.

Best of all, there was a variety of work for the young doctor, and he threw himself into it with characteristic energy. By his tireless devotion to his duties he won great popularity with the miners and their wives. By living close to the people, he came to know them well. "Beneath their dark and upright dignity," he wrote, "the people were, at heart, warm and kindly" (144). These figures, together with the settings and the future author, appear in the novels and are given full-scale treatment. They supplied him with a dramatic cast of characters, a ready-made network of complex relationships, and a complete set of thunderous emotions. In all of this he was not only an active participant but, as the trusted doctor, an advantaged spectator. Ten years later he would portray young Andrew Manson, hero of *The Citadel,* thrown into an emotional turmoil by an analogous situation.

Years of medical studies and two years of struggling to live on a relatively meager income began to seem like years of drudgery. Whatever work difficulties Cronin had to contend with, there was still the unavoidable matter of how he was to earn enough. During a particularly gray frustrating period in his life, when the impulse to succeed was more powerful than ever, another idea took hold of him: he would study for three major postgraduate degrees. To do this he had to borrow books from the Royal Society of London and sit up nights studying after he had finished his rounds. The nearest laboratory where he could work to qualify for the new degrees was in Cardiff, more than fifty miles away. Cronin bought a secondhand motorcycle and rode there once a week. He formed the habit of working for two hours at the laboratory, then speeding back home "to find myself faced with a surgery case in the kitchen when I returned" (164). This schedule did not leave as much time as he wished to spend with May, but he sacrificed his personal pleasure for duty.

The examinations he had to take in London for the degrees were so difficult that three out of four candidates usually failed. Cronin passed with honors and found himself not only with an M.D., but also with the M.R.C.P. (Member of the Royal College of Physicians) and the D.Ph. Later, he took examinations for a post with the Ministry of Mines, came in first, and in 1924 secured an appointment as medical inspector of mines, which took him all over England. "I had some times," he said, "to crawl on my hands and knees—and the mine no more than a rabbit warren, dripping water, jagged rocks above it—half a mile from the pit shelf."[13] Out of this experience he wrote and published in 1926 and 1927 two significant studies: *Report on Dust Inhalation in Haematite Mines* and *Investigations in First-Aid Organization at Collieries in Great Britain.* The outcome of his journeys to investigate the conditions said to prevail in these mining communities is the picture of *The Stars Look Down* and *The Citadel.*

Meanwhile, because his savings turned out to be far too little for the kind of London practice he had dreamed about, in 1926 he had to buy a place in a rundown section of Bayswater, London. Mrs. Cronin recalled the next three years as the worst period through which they ever lived. The house was large, about half-furnished; a big obligation was due to Dr. Herbert Tanner, who had sold them the practice; an infant son was born in Tredeger and another was on the way—and no money. The Cronins ate salt herring and potatoes, skimped on coal, and had to call in the plumber to repair frozen water pipes.

Nevertheless, young Dr. Cronin was on his own at last, and he began his career as a doctor and tried to make some money as well. At the very moment when it appeared morbidly possible to Cronin that he might have doomed himself to a future of hardship, one of life's inexplicable strokes of chance steered his fortunes upward. He was called in, purely for emergency reasons, to attend wealthy Mrs. Arbuthnot. Well aware of his good fortune, he knew intuitively that he stood at one of life's crossroads, and he pressed the advantage for all that it was worth. He was, he assures us, "a great rogue" at this period (197). In her wake came an avalanche of well-to-do patients, and his savings grew. For these wealthy patients he invented an ailment named "asthenia"—which means no more than "weakness or general debility" (196). Then he "cured" his patients with high-priced injections: "Again and yet again my sharp and shining needle sank into fashionable buttocks, bared upon the finest linen sheets. I became expert, indeed, superlative, in the art of penetrating the worst end of the best society" (197). His liaison with these "idle, spoiled, and neurotic" patients (196) gave him insight into a world of which hitherto he had been perforce innocent: it was a world where people spent money like water. He got them to talk about their private lives; their recollections, like everything else Cronin encountered, made their way into his work.

The poor doctor was now an image of the past. At the end of three years he had paid off his predecessor, furnished his home, bought a car, and employed house servants. By 1930 he was still living in Bayswater but attending a good many patients in London's more fashionable parts. Getting to that point from a poverty-ridden boyhood in Scotland had been an epic triumph. He could hardly believe that he was out of debt, making money, and better yet, achieving recognition in his profession. All that he had dreamed, planned, worked for so industriously, was, it seemed, becoming reality. He now had sufficient economic stability to be able to do more or less whatever he wished with his life.

But Cronin's success as a physician also fed his vanity and increased his self-indulgence. " 'I think I liked you better in those hobnail boots,' his wife told him. 'You thought more of your cases and less of your guineas when you wore them' "

(199). Indeed, quite apart from his financial success, Cronin discovered within himself the seeds of dissatisfaction with the character of his practice:

> More and more I was preoccupied by my "high-class" patients, less and less by the ordinary working people who came to the side door. While I enjoyed the sweets of prosperity and revelled in the sense of fulfilled ambition—nothing is more thrilling to the Scot than the knowledge that he is "getting on"—I could not but contrast the work I was doing now with the work I had once done. (198)

Also at work was an urge to write about the patients and the experiences of a physician. He thought of this desire off and on throughout the months following, but only to the point of saying to his wife: "You know, I believe I could write a novel if I had the time" (252). Such a notion is not uncommon to perceptive young men who dream of fame through accomplishment. For most it remains only a fantasy. For Cronin the dream was to come true: he didn't realize then that he was soon to have more time on his hands than he planned.

The Novelist (1930–81)

Henceforth the progression of Cronin's life is, for us, mainly the story of his books. Theoretically, his inauspicious origins and early environment should not only have militated against his succeeding but could have foredoomed him to obscurity. He possessed no money, no friends in power, no family tradition in letters. Still, with every disadvantage apparently massed against him, Cronin by the force of his own will and his dogged persistence eventually burst through all barriers. In retrospect, his life can be seen as a succession of right decisions—the right school, the right wife, the right career, and now finally, about to give up a prestigious practice to work as an author, the right course for the truth seeker to follow.

From a literary point of view, then, 1930 is the most significant date in Cronin's life. In that year the combination of two realities brought the decision to close up his office and go away for a vacation. One reason was the increasing boredom he was experiencing in his work, which had become a bureaucratic office routine with a few house calls. More ominous was that either because of working too hard in London, or because of too many pressures, his health was beginning to suffer. A colleague diagnosed a chronic duodenal ulcer and ordered a complete rest for the young doctor. It meant throwing away everything for which he had struggled. There was no alternative.

Without telling his wife the reason, and without asking for her advice, Cronin sold his practice, moved to Dalchena Farm, near Inverary, and announced that he was going to become a novelist: "I want to write a book, have always wanted to. It is something I must get out of my system" (254). He had nothing to lose. Even if the book were returned with the usual rejection slip, he would have the satisfaction of knowing that three months of his stay had been filled with a task that had absorbed him. He would also find unlimited time for quiet meditation, broken only by the hum of insects, the chorus of singing birds.

While his wife and two sons swam and fished in the nearby lake, the doctor isolated himself in a cold attic room where he worked mainly by candlelight. His industry was astonishing. With the same mood of mingled desperation and sheer willpower that he had felt as a struggling medical student, he tried to pour out his pent-up thoughts in twopenny notebooks. The first day he stared at a blank page for three hours. The next day and the days that followed were torturous for him, but at last the novel began to take shape. At first his rate of progress was about eight hundred words a day. By the end of the second month he was writing two thousand words a day. He worked frantically, writing hour by hour, then lying asleep in bed, then rising to switch on the light and read through what he had written during the day. Meanwhile, nature was restoring his health.

At the end of two months the novel was half-written, but when he took time out to read the finished chapters, he was disgusted. With characteristic impulsiveness he threw the manuscript into the ash can and started out broodingly for a walk in the rain. He had never dreamed that writing fiction could make so much demand on a man's heart and soul. But a Scots farmer laboriously digging a ditch upon which his father had worked before him taught Cronin the lesson that saved that valuable manuscript. The fact that two generations of men had worked patiently in the hope that some day a little pasture might be drained made Cronin see how rash and impatient he had been. He went back to his writing, and after another month of white-heat work the novel was finished. In three months he had written 250,000 words. Cronin wrote to two well-considered publishers. One replied that he would be "pleased" to consider the typescript, the other replied that he would be "very pleased." Cronin sent it to the second, Victor Gollancz, and his career as a novelist was decisively launched. He had wisely followed his sudden impulse.

After the climactic events of medical practice and his long climb to financial security and professional success, Cronin's sudden transition to a best-selling author of fiction seems somehow anticlimactic. Less fortunate authors, remembering the years of hard work and disappointment, the heartaches of failure after failure before a salable novel is written, and the long struggle to achieve recognition, might envy him the ease with which he made the transition from physician to author. In glowing health and at peace with the world and himself, his life soon settled into a disciplined routine of reading, writing, and traveling. *Hatter's Castle* established him both critically and financially, and a long string of best-sellers followed. He was soon besieged by invitations, and he began to move in circles of political power and influence. Like many new authors who suddenly leap into prominence, he actually began to meet on equal terms with the company he had always read about. Those who knew him personally were quite convinced of his talent. He was a witty and vivid talker, a man of warmth and charm, of intelligence, immensely wide-ranging interests, and profound curiosity.

Although Cronin enjoyed all the normal pleasures of London life—the theater, suits from Savile Row, auction sales of art and antiques, watching cricket at Lords, and playing golf, a game at which he won several trophies—he remained somewhat lacking in self-assurance; he never felt, throughout his life, fully at ease in fashionable society, and he was always sensitive about his impoverished childhood. Many of his novels show evidence of strong class feeling, the selfishness and triviality of the upper class being unfavorably contrasted with the sincerity and altruism of ordinary people, especially the rural poor.

Helped by the successful filming of several of his novels,

including *The Citadel,* Cronin had built up his American market. In 1939, foreseeing a war in which he was too old to serve usefully as a combatant, he moved with his family (there were now three sons) to New England, where he was to make his home happily for seventeen years, and where in 1941 he achieved a great critical and commercial success with *The Keys of the Kingdom*—written in a boxroom on the top of a frame house in York Village, without heating and himself wrapped up in blankets.

But success and fame are never free to those who gain them, and they seem to have extorted an unusually high price from Cronin. Although this success woke fresh and vivid images within the novelist's creative imagination, they also threatened to force his moral and humane sympathies into a crisis of conscience. At the height of financial prosperity and great reputation, in good health and with his work flowing smoothly and abundantly, Cronin felt a deep malaise, "a feeling of emptiness and dissatisfaction" (269). He was not exhausted, not defeated, but suddenly emptied and left feeling naked and exposed. For the first time in his life he had the "leisure to undertake some meditative occupation" (279), with the following results:

I saw myself, with a sombre inner eye, as completely insincere, the betrayer of a principle I had never recognised before. It was a singular paradox. For years, driven by that thirsting and insatiable demon, that desire for success, implanted by my early penury, forced on by the less worthy element of my personality, I had sought relentlessly, step by step, the golden apples of the Hesperides, gift of Gaea to Hera, and now that the fruit was within my grasp, all ready to be plucked, I saw it suddenly as dross, a lure both tawdry and worthless. . . . And more, I began dimly to discern how much attention I had paid to the wrong things in life, and how little to the right. (268–69)

After struggling for all that fame and fortune could bring him, it is ironic that Cronin now had a far more pressing matter on his mind than worldly success. For years he had ignored matters of the spirit; then, almost coinciding with the end of one career and the start of a new, even more successful one, he found himself confronted with a fundamental fact of existence. He had been born a Catholic, observing the outward practice of his faith. May had become a Catholic, too. But he had drifted gradually into a position where religion was something entirely outside his inner experience.

In the years after World War II he took his wife on pilgrimages to Vienna, Italy, and France, in particular Normandy, and experienced what might be called an epiphany. In war-battered Europe they met the kind of people Erich Maria Remarque wrote about in *Spark of Life* (1928): they saw people without homes, food, or money, but with an "indestructible" human spirit (293). Each trip provided experiences that further crystallized Cronin's maturing faith. In other cities this conviction grew, but with it the question: "How can this Divine Being be credible . . . in the face of a tormented world?" (325) This question intensified as the days passed, until he answered it by quoting Thomas à Kempis: "So long as suffering appears grievous to thee and thou seekest to fly from it, so long will it be ill with thee and the tribulation from which thou fliest will everywhere follow thee" (325). By accepting pain, disappointment, and misfortune, "we survive the supreme test of submission to the will of God" (325).

His return to the Catholic faith was momentous. With à Kempis, Cronin moved from the rebellious phase with all its suggestions of ambition, cleverness, and self-development, to the opposite ideals—self-sacrifice, mortification of self, and renunciation of the joys of the world. "Of one thing I am convinced," he wrote. "Nothing, no philosophy, no power on earth will restore our shocked and battered world except the teaching of Him who bore to Golgotha the burden of all mankind" (330). These thoughts gave him deep contentment. And why not? Like Dante, this young author had lost his way in the dark forest and found it again.

We have seen that Cronin had a rich background into which he would reach for ideas for his books. The Glasgow medical school environment; the touch-and-go associations with mental patients at a suburban asylum; the medical practice in a Welsh mining village with its calls in the night and impromptu surgery on the kitchen tables and in mine shafts; the drama, pathos, and cynical worldliness that passed under his eyes as a medical practitioner in London—all these episodes were used as material for his novels. Cronin was essentially a moralist and a man of feeling, deeply moved by human suffering especially if it was caused by deliberate injustice or wanton cruelty. He believed in order; he believed in people acting decently and humanely in the particular rank of life to which they were called. Perhaps his wide experience in watching the suffering of others, his own struggles, and his keen insight into character helped him to develop a philosophy of "live-and-let-live."

The richest source of material for his novels, however, was his newfound faith. This is particularly true in the later novels, beginning with *The Keys of the Kingdom.* The source of his renewed strength can be summed up in a few words: "No matter how we try to escape, to lose ourselves [from our divine source], there is no substitute for God" (328). This is a simple statement of sincere faith by a man whose adventures in various environments were marked by a steady development in spirit and art.

Chapter Two

The Early Phase:
A Divided World

The unhappy fate of the men or women whom choice or chance has alienated from the human community greatly interested Cronin. In his early novels—*Hatter's Castle* (1931), *Three Loves* (1932), and *Grand Canary* (1933)—he explores the moral and philosophical implications of the theme, and out of them he begins to evolve a doctrine of social community as an ideal to set opposite the isolated individual. This positive doctrine is implicit in his delineation of individuals who, because of the accidents of birth or character or action or achievement, were set apart from normal human relationships. These persons may appropriately be called *Isolatoes,* a term coined by Herman Melville when he described in *Moby Dick* the crew of the Pequod: "They were nearly all Islanders. . . . *Isolatoes* too, I call such, not acknowledging the common continent of men, but each *Isolato* living on a separate continent of his own."[1] In Cronin's novels one character at least is just such an exile. Whereas James Brodie and Lucy Moore succumb as involuntary victims, Harvey Leith escapes at last into a social environment congenial to himself.

Hatter's Castle

"I have great pleasure in announcing the sudden and most surprising arrival in England of a new and most important author."[2] So Hugh Walpole, himself a successful middlebrow writer, opened his review of *Hatter's Castle* in the *New York Herald-Tribune.* Walpole's admiration for Cronin's first novel— the "finest" since the war—was a promise of the response to come from both sides of the Atlantic. The *Spectator* called the novel "a big achievement, . . . brutal, violent, and full of life."[3] The London *Times Literary Supplement* praised Cronin's "force of description, strong human sympathy and deep knowledge of the persons and scenes from which it is drawn."[4] James Agate, writing for the New York *Daily Express,* called it "Epoch-making."[5] Percy Hutchinson in the *New York Times* proclaimed that it was "the work of a novelist who is destined for the seats of the mighty."[6] By general agreement, *Hatter's Castle* was deemed a powerful work of "individuality and integrity."[7]

To develop the plot, Cronin uses the familiar Victorian conventions available to all aspiring writers of the time: a straightforward linear chronology (with occasional flashbacks) unfolded through the agency of the omniscient third-person narrator; a propensity toward stereotype characters all of whom move through stock situations; with an emphasis on melodrama and Gothic horror. What is more, the novel is divided into three books (or acts) and follows the time-honored pattern in a well-made play: exposition, complication, climax, and denouement. Each chapter is a separate, dramatically rendered scene, composed of action, dialogue, narration, and authorial comment, and usually set off in the action by the entrance of one or more characters. Moreover, each chapter (and book) ends with an impending crisis in order to arouse interest in subsequent chapters. Cronin's strong tendency to think in graphic dramaturgical terms is evident in all of his novels.

Added to these conventions is one of the most familiar themes of Greek tragedy: the retribution that attends overweening pride. James Brodie is one of many in a long tradition of fictional overreachers, characters who are destroyed not by metaphysical agency—as God expelled Adam and Eve from Eden or Mephistopheles collected his share of the bargain—but by his own nature and the consequences of living in and rejecting human community. In *Hatter's Castle,* therefore, we see embodied the seeds of one of Cronin's central themes: Brodie becomes a fearful symbol of the self-enclosed individualism that, carried to its furthest extreme, brings disaster both upon himself and the group of which he is a part.

The story begins in the small northern Scottish town of Levenford, on the Firth of Clyde, during the last quarter of the nineteenth century. In the region adjacent to the open country stands the last house on the road—an absurd model of a Scottish castle—and here most of the action occurs. Its owner, James Brodie, is a man whose inordinate self-love and unusually strong physique have made him the most feared person in town as well as the tyrant of a trembling household. He has deluded himself into believing that his hat shop is a thriving business, that his house is a romantic castle, and that he himself is related to the aristocracy. The novel proceeds almost consecutively from its beginning, with the hero at the "peak" of his powers, to his decline into futility, frustration, and, finally, alienation.

The driving force of the book, however, is the portrayal of the successive disasters that Brodie brings upon himself and his family. Margaret, his feeble, downtrodden wife, is reduced to abjection and dies horribly of cancer. Mary, his elder daughter, is a lovely, gentle girl not quite able to cope with her father. She becomes pregnant, is thrown out of the house into a raging storm, and eventually marries the young doctor whom Brodie hates. Nessie, the younger daughter, is driven to insanity and suicide by Brodie's morbid determination that she shall win a scholarship and go on to college. Matthew, the weakling son who is under pressure to succeed as a salesman, robs his mother, lies to both of his parents, and runs off with his father's mistress, Nancy. By the end of the novel, therefore, any manifestations of Brodie's supposed supremacy have vanished. Not only has he lost his family, but he has lost his business and descended into alcohol and debauchery. He is left shattered, with no companion but his tragic, greedy old mother, and with no hope but death.

This, then, is Cronin's first novel: savage, violent, sentimental, extravagant. From the beginning of his literary career he was noted for his sheer brute ability as a teller of tales rather than for any distinctive "literary" qualities of form or style; but therein lies his strength. The story's impact is disturbing, and the reasons for the effect produced on several generations of readers are easy to analyze.[8] Admittedly, the story line is both action-packed and tragedy-laden, and that fact must have accounted for a good deal of the novel's popularity. Mary's plight as she falls in love, becomes pregnant, then is driven from home, constitutes a familiar scene in literature with which readers could identify. The spectacle of Brodie's treachery also must have stirred the emotions of Cronin's readers. But the book's popularity was due also to the incidentals of the story—the atmosphere, the mystery, the horror. In *Hatter's Castle,* as in most Victorian fiction, Cronin's use of setting discloses the primary characteristics of his created world.

Woven through the book are patterns of developing images and symbols that serve important structural functions: they relate and unify the individual lives presented in the book; they support and embody its themes; and they are the means by which the texture of an event or feeling is conveyed. One cluster of these images grows out of the title, which refers, of course, literally to the house, and also to James Brodie himself and his career. The "castle," at once a physical structure and symbol of the Brodie family, is pictured in the first chapter in terms that both symbolize its owner's conspicuous difference and detachment from the community and prophesy the dreadful development and outcome of the story:

> Its grandiose architecture contained some quality which restrained merriment, some deeper, lurking, more perverse motive, sensed upon intensive scrutiny, which lay about the house like a deformity and stood within its very structure like a violation of truth in stone.[9]

That a crisis has been brewing for some time is made evident with additional descriptive passages, all of which emphasize that Brodie's castle is a place of gloom and solitude, "more fitted for a prison than a home" (140), "veiled, forbidding, sinister; its purpose likewise hidden and obscure" (5). Cronin compares the front of the house to "an animal upon its deep-dug paws" (4) and to "a broad frowning forehead disfigured by a deep grooved stigma" (5). The pompous dignity of the gables greets the visitor with "cold severity" (4). The parapet embraces the body of the house like a "manacle"; its windows are "secret, close-set eyes [which] grudgingly" admit light; its doorway is "a thin repellent mouth" (5). From this description we sense the animal power and the amorality that characterize the image of the house. We feel the threat of something unreasoning and unrevealed. Not only does this description provide a haunting counterpoint to the action of *Hatter's Castle,* but also it establishes the essential character of Brodie well before he appears, before he is even named.

The members of the Brodie family share with the house a

condition of imminent collapse. Typical of so many novelists, Cronin's device, here and elsewhere, is to put his minor characters in dire straits at the outset of the action so that they can be tested against the hardships life has to offer. In the first chapter he chooses the human device of an imaginary visitor to present the scene. He moves slowly from the outlying vicinity to the exterior of the castle itself, and then through a kitchen window and on into the room with which he is concerned. The effect is of a slow quasi-cinematic focusing in on the presentation of the four characters. Having established the setting, Cronin then introduces the family members as they wait for Brodie. He moves from grandmother to elder daughter, from younger daughter to mother, and each picture is presented as a miniature scene in a continuous drama of frustration. We see the gluttonous grandmother scold Mary for her forgetfulness. Mary, lost in thought of her new boyfriend, ignores the old woman's admonition that she avoid sitting in her father's special chair. We see Margaret, untidy, with an expression of abnegation on her "worn, tired and pathetic" face. Mother and daughter seem "alien and unrelated" (9). All along, we note a strange absence of the usual signs of domesticity in a large country household, including the caring friends, the nurtured child, the affectionate servant, the all-providing father. Like the house itself, their lives leave an impression of darkness, crowdedness, and oppressiveness.

But this scene, which opens the novel, is more than a battle of wills. It is the dramatist's method—and Cronin is very much the playwright in conceiving his scenes—of preparing the background and battleground that are to give the ensuing themes and conflicts their validity. Thus the scene dramatized in this first chapter is a miniature of the entire novel.

Along with the mood, therefore, the setting of *Hatter's Castle* functions also as a complement to the characterization. The castle symbolizes Brodie himself and becomes an immutable prophecy that he will never again be anything else, no matter what fantasies of educational, social, or economic success cloud his mind. For Brodie is a man motivated almost exclusively by a pragmatism. Concern for his own personal welfare and success shows itself in two strong characteristics: his dominant animality, which instinctively and meanly desires its own pleasure; and his insensitive amorality, which shows no twinge of conscience or sacred dictation of moral responsibility. Brodie's selfish moral isolation preserves him untamed and untaught in his human contacts and in his civilizing pursuits.

To reinforce our association of Brodie with the castle, Cronin draws upon analogies with violent, savage animals. Most of the animals are wild, and strength is equal to brutishness. Brodie is likened to an "angry bull" (137), a "ravenous animal" (213), a "sleeping lion" (266), a "restless leviathan" (294), a "caged tiger" (380). A variety of verbs also suggest in him a physical recoil from human contact: he roars like "an angry ram" (48), attacks his food "wolfishly" (215), broods, sneers, and casts recriminative glances (13). Although occasionally Brodie could regret the cold isolation his monomania produces, most of the time he deliberately spurns as far as possible the assistance of other human agents. Proudly he boasts: "You're a proud man, Brodie, . . . and by God! you have reason to be" (132). But the fate Cronin assigns to this individualist is total defeat.

Cronin also uses physical deformity as a macabre sign of insane depravity. Brodie's very appearance, for example, sets him aside from the mainstream of humanity. He belongs to the Byronic heroes (or Satanic / Miltonic)—those hero-villains beginning with *Paradise Lost* who are not the more admired on moral grounds, but who remain the most powerful in terms of their effect upon the reader:

His head was massive, his grey eyes small and deep set, his jaw hard and so resolutely muscular that as he chewed, large firm knobs rose up and subsided rhythmically under the smooth brown jowl. The face itself was broad and strong and would have been noble but for the insufficient depth of the forehead and the narrow spacing of the eyes. A heavy brown moustache covered his upper lip, partly hiding the mouth; but beneath this glossy mask his lower lip protruded with a full and sullen arrogance. (11)

In all externals Brodie has stepped straight from the popular lowbrow theater: he is villainously deformed. From the evidence of the novel, Brodie is his own worst enemy: his choleric temper, his arrogant pride in possessions and position, his excessive attention to Nancy (and his equally ill-bred abuse of Margaret), his chilling presence on his children, culminating in Nessie's tragic death. Brodie becomes almost a fairy-tale ogre, the only specimen of the kind in Cronin's works (unless Richard Barras in *The Stars Look Down* is a counterpart). Cronin also carries into this stock picture of unmitigated malice a genuinely powerful suggestion of obsessively compulsive behavior. Brodie's action in beating Mary, his repeated angry outbursts, and his cruel treatment of his other children are insane. Psychological stress and abnormality were matters of lifelong interest to Cronin. Brodie's meanness with his phony culture and pretensions to cleverness reminds us of another of Cronin's favorite books— Georges Bernanos's *La Joie* (1929). Like the French novelist, Cronin is offering a particularly tantalizing story: the man who is free from moral restraint becomes evil, beastlike, brutish, subhuman it seems.

The mood of amoral indifference that is associated with the castle and that has a prominent place in the portrayal of the hatter's true self would seem at first to contradict any claim that a tragic atmosphere pervades the novel. Strictly speaking, tragedy can occur only to a character who is morally responsible, to a being who is capable of performing human acts, of choosing deliberately between good and bad actions. In the strict Aristotelian and Shakespearean senses this is true. But if we may here loosely define tragedy as a pathetic condition of privation, a moral incapacity for living in a totally human manner, then James Brodie is a tragic figure. However, by no means does he suffer any downfall that he recognizes. He is not a victim of the treachery of others. He is what he is throughout the novel. The fear engendered by the novel is not aroused by contemplation of Brodie's final outcome, but rather by prediction of the heartache and pain he causes (or will cause) those who have anything to do with him.

Brodie's victims, once conceived, are introduced with a minimum of biography or "prehistory." Cronin draws attention to their facial expressions, their eyes, their smiles, their ways of looking at or not looking at another person, and above all the impressions they make on one another. In Mary, Margaret, and Nessie the extraordinary quality of Cronin's powers of characterization is particularly apparent.

To develop Mary's conflict with her father, Cronin draws

from the dramatic tradition of the sentimental or domestic tragedy in which the conflict centers around parental approval or disapproval of the children's marriage partners. Like the typical Victorian heroine, Mary is more than pretty: her face shows animation, intelligence, and character. Her soft brown eyes sparkle, twinkle, or shine, and they subtly reveal love she wants to hide, anger she tries to overcome, and merriment she should suppress. Her mouth is "sensitive"; her skin is like "the smooth soft texture of petals of magnolia" (8). Her complexion is clear and white, and the color in her cheeks deepens with exercise, excitement, or embarrassment. The rest of her body is modestly ignored, although an occasional white column of neck or turn of the ankle is seen.

But slight deviations from the norm serve as clues to an individualized heroine. She defies her grandmother by sitting in her father's favorite seat; she argues with Brodie in defense of Denis Foyle's honor; she disobeys her father's orders against meeting Foyle at the Levenford fair. Thus while Mary fits a given category, she ultimately escapes the confines of the typical. Unlike Margaret and Nessie, she fights back against the circumstances and people that have trampled on her. She refuses to destroy herself voluntarily (unlike Nessie) and is rewarded at the novel's end with a happy marriage. Like other girls powerless before a tyrannical father, Mary expects to find comparative freedom in her marriage.

Both Margaret and Nessie, on the other hand, fit the stock Victorian role of the martyr or traditional sufferer who bears the indignities and tortures of her life with the self-sacrificial grace and patient fortitude of a Griselda, and whose life ends in pain or early death. Physical description early in the novel suggests their respective roles. Margaret walks with a "shuffling gait, taking short flurried steps with her body inclined forward, so that . . . she appeared always to be in a hurry and fearful of being late." Her hair "straggled untidily about her face," and her face is "worn, tired and pathetic: her aspect bowed and drooping" (9). She carries her head to one side "to exhibit resignation and true Christian submission in periods of trial or tribulation" (7).

Nessie, too, is unbelievably submissive. Her hair is "flaxen," her eyes are "light" and "inoffensive" and show always the "soft placating expression which gave her the appearance of endeavouring continually to please" (10). Suggestions of Nessie as ingenue are made when Cronin tells us: "Her face was narrow with a high delicate white forehead, pink waxen doll's cheeks, a thin pointed chin and a small mouth, parted perpetually by the drooping of her lower lip, all expressive, as was her present soft, void smile, of the same immature and ingenuous, but none the less innate weakness" (10). Compared to Brodie's volcanic, predatory character, both Margaret and Nessie are quiet, rather shadowy figures.

To emphasize further their roles as victims, Cronin identifies the heroines with the domestic and gentler animals. Margaret is compared either to a "poor weak sheep" (266) or to a "submissive dog" (286). At times she feels "hunted" (266); her cry is like that of an "outraged animal" (164). Nessie is a "young foal" (96), a "little white mouse" (535). Other animals are used throughout the novel to symbolize the girls' destiny. Their catastrophes have a quasi-tragic inevitability that comes from the desperate actions of the trapped animal escaping her cage. This image is insistently and consistently patterned throughout the novel.

In the sympathetic portrayal of Margaret's and Nessie's lives and in the suggestion that their devotion to Brodie *is* enslavement (at least partly self-induced), Cronin reveals his concern with the conditions—economic, social, and psychological—that lead to such a life. What is more, such extensive use of imagery in *Hatter's Castle* serves to heighten the novel by a very full exploitation of the pictorial possibilities of the story; it is a means by which Cronin develops such themes as the battle between good and evil and the corruption of innocence. Through his heroines, Cronin shows innocence set in a corrupt world where only the appearances of a Victorian morality remain. Imagery functions powerfully as a method of defining both character and theme.

One other character type remains: the player of bit parts who fits a traditional role. Grandma Brodie, for example, is the eternal invalid. She is peevish and greedy, querulous and interfering. Her physical features indicate her temperament: her body is "shriveled and knotted like the bole of a sapless tree, dried but still hard and resilient"; her hands are "gnarled"; her face is colored like "a withered leaf"; her hair is parted in the middle, "showing a straight white furrow of scalp, and drawn tight into a hard knot behind" (6–7). Matthew, on the other hand, is the conventional weakling of nineteenth-century sentimental fiction. Weak, effeminate, and overly sensitive, he is the victim of much of his father's derision and sadism. Nancy the barmaid typifies the Dark Lady of Victorian literature. Unlike Margaret, she is neither subservient nor serviceable. To the mother's intimations of fertility, she opposes a sterile and haughty beauty. To the ideal of subjection, she offers a cynicism that ridicules male supremacy. Margaret, as the typical Victorian wife, finds the fulfillment of her destiny in abnegating certain aspects of her personality. The Dark Lady, on the other hand, replenishes her personality through establishing intellectual, creative, and even sexual superiority over the male. Brodie wilts under such treatment.

Also noteworthy here is Cronin's interest in medicine. From *Hatter's Castle* on, down to his most recent novels, he brings doctors into the foreground of his narratives to reveal both a deep and versatile knowledge of their calling and a lasting concern for their personal histories. He is also comfortable with their techniques. In his abuse of Mary, for example, Dr. Laurie foreshadows Doctors Hampton, Ivory, and Freedman in *The Citadel*. In them we see how science, in its cold quest for facts, tends to destroy beauty and to ignore human feeling. Dr. Laurie, as we are introduced to him in the episodes with Mary, is not a particularly heroic or attractive figure. He is a conventional practitioner with a sharp eye for the dollar. He defers to his social superiors and snubs his inferiors. He is a useful person, though hardly a noble one.

Dr. Renwick, on the other hand, foreshadows the kindness and idealism represented by Andrew Manson, also in *The Citadel*. He typifies the highly trained and immensely skillful specialist who is yet a well-rounded human being. He treats his patients as human beings, keeps up with the times, employs modern methods, and contributes to the community in which he works. Certainly one of the admirable aspects of *Hatter's Castle* is Cronin's presentation of the problems relating to medicine. He gives concretely both sides of this question with thoroughness and fairness.

Although critics agree that in *Hatter's Castle* the author creates a powerfully compelling story, and although he deals seriously and vigorously with important ideas, it is less certain that he has shaped these ideas into an entirely satisfactory novel. Cronin himself, after its appearance, did not make excessive claim for the book. *Hatter's Castle,* as he maintained in a letter to Hugh Walpole, was a "very clumsy beginning" written to please himself and sent to Gollancz with but "a shadowy hope for publication."[10] The title, for example, suggests a literary origin for the author's imagination; and no doubt the central figure of Brodie owes something to Dickens and a good deal to Hardy—though with little of his irony. Brodie's inordinate self-love, the driving force of both his life and the book, is presented with clinical thoroughness in its effect on his own life and on the lives of the other characters. But his aberration is inadequately explained or motivated, and this lack robs the whole book of meaning. Why is Brodie so horrible? Was he the victim of child abuse? What was his relationship with his father? Are Cronin's inferences of illegitimacy to be taken seriously? Without answers to these questions, the book borders on a case history of abnormality. Lack of motivation for his character is the novel's most serious flaw.

Another difficulty with *Hatter's Castle* is that Brodie provides a center for the novel without becoming a "hero," in this way somewhat like Emily Brontë's Heathcliff (in *Wuthering Heights,* 1847) and Samuel Richardson's Robert Lovelace (in *Clarissa,* 1747–48). Cronin's character is neither sympathetic nor realistic; rather, he is a figure from an unsentimental melodrama. In any novel we need somebody with whom we can sympathize. Brodie is surely an object more of pity, if even that, than of tragedy. His is an ironic end.

To these counts against the novel may be added the weak drawing of some of the minor characters. Brodie's son, Matthew, is a predictable character in much of the plot development. Margaret, too, is a willful, weak heroine who never stands up for her rights, no matter how brutally Brodie treats her. She is monotonously and unbelievably good, generous to the point of self-sacrifice, quiet, forgiving, and capable of absolutely selfless love. She is so self-effacing and gentle that she becomes an abstraction of an ideal rather than a character who realistically represents a human being. But perhaps it is sufficient that these characters and others remain stereotypes, since Cronin's main point is that they are pawns of Brodie's.

Perhaps another legitimate criticism of the plot is that the sheer number of misfortunes suffered by Brodie and his family seems excessive and implausible. Possibly, but it is part of Cronin's philosophy that troubles never come singly, and certainly all of Brodie's misfortunes can be traced to his character and actions. "Character is Fate," quotes Thomas Hardy in *The Mayor of Casterbridge* (1886); and nemesis works unerringly through Brodie's own glaring defects. Imaginative belief in Brodie himself compels belief in what happens to him.

Victorian fiction depends above all on the profound appeal of its characters. The Victorian novelists rely on their representation of men and women to engage their readers and establish shared sympathies and aversions. By using their characters to bring out each reader's elementary need for identification and dissociation, the novelists are able to share gratifying wishes and defenses with their public. Cronin, too, relies essentially on characterization to mold our points of view and bring them in contact with his implied beliefs. He lets his figures think, act, and speak for themselves, yet also tells us through the voice of his narrator what our attitudes ought to be.

In conclusion, we often hear of Cronin as one of the most "cinematic" of the English novelists, and by that a number of different things appears to be meant. There are the stunning atmospheric effects and the broadly environmental areas, from the evocation of the castle to the description of the storm rendered at the end of Book 1, which any ambitious cinematographer or director would be challenged to transfer to film. Then there is the intense dwelling on physical detail, and Cronin's interest in conveying a complex thematic meaning through such devices. But Cronin's roots in melodrama did not leave him with a superficial taste for violent action. Although *Hatter's Castle* is in many ways a conventional novel, there are ideas, themes, and techniques in it that reappear in Cronin's later, more mature work. The characters are typical of Cronin: paradoxical mixtures of good and bad, weak and strong. Possessiveness, to the point of the pathological, is used as a catalyst to introduce a conflict and action, and, as in his later novels, it is always expressly condemned. The unrequited love theme, which appears so often in Cronin's writing, is present in the form of Mary's plight. Also, the central idea of rebellion against social pressures anticipates the kinds of revolt that motivate so many Cronin characters—including artists, seekers, and criminals. Above all, we see in this novel evidence of Cronin's serious interest in the action of the mind under stress. In his next novel, *Three Loves,* he develops that interest by turning to the psychological implications of possessive love.

Three Loves

Hatter's Castle was in many ways a happy accident, securing for its author laudatory reviews and substantial earnings and establishing him as a writer of great promise. In its hero, readers found an outstanding personality: a hatter in Levenford, in strongly characterized surroundings, who lives through a destiny of suffering and tragedy. Readers were also treated to a return to the English novel in the grand tradition. Its themes—the rejected family, the struggle against poverty, the desire for wealth, the consequences of possessive or unrequited love, the pain of loneliness—recur throughout Cronin's fiction.

Prompted by that success and by a sense of ever-increasing power and confidence, Cronin went to work on his second novel, *Three Loves,* trying to capitalize on his artistic strengths while overcoming what he perceived to be major stylistic weaknesses:

My second book, I wrote on the Sussex Downs, where I have a little country place. Like the landscape, it is more even, less exaggerated. I was seething with ideas all the time, but I kept a firm hand—poured the tumult into a smoother mold. I felt at the time that I had been deliberately restrained in writing that book, and I think that I got rid of the ponderous verbosity of *Hatter's Castle.*[11]

Within two months after the publication of *Three Loves* Cronin had received a number of encouraging reviews. F. T. Marsh claimed the novel as "a more genuine piece of work"[12] than *Hatter's Castle;* Gerald Bullett called it a book that "commands respect,"[13] although he was only the first of several people to point out that it would have been better for being shorter. Other reviews were also enthusiastic—the *Springfield Republican*

finding the novel an improvement in technique and characterization,[14] the *Nation* speaking of it as "a swiftly moving, pitiful
and always interesting story"[15]—and Cronin must have been
especially pleased by the sympathetic review of Lucy Moore's
situation in the London *Times Literary Supplement:*

> Dr. Cronin has one great gift of the novelist by vocation, that of
> seeing his characters with entire clarity in all their goings out and
> their comings in. Another of his gifts is that of ruthlessly going through
> to the end. His stories are not simply elaborated sketches but are
> brought to a finish of tragic completeness and death.[16]

In the *Spectator* of 27 February, however, the reviewer—
L. A. G. Strong—declared that Lucy's character is not worth the
592 pages devoted to her, that she lacks the "charm and strength
of character to justify Dr. Cronin's indefatigable pursuit [and
that] Cronin's reputation must rest, for the present at any rate,
upon his first book."[17] Yet the book attracted and held the
rapt attention of many intelligent and discriminating readers;
and in complexity of thought it ranks distinctively higher than
Hatter's Castle.

Like its predecessor, *Three Loves* is set in the Scottish Lowlands,
among the petty bourgeoisie to whom social position is all-im-
portant. Its heroine, Lucy Moore, reminds us of James Brodie
for two reasons: she is determined to eradicate something she
believes to be evil, and she is proudly self-reliant, wanting self-
respect, honor, and distinction in society. She is ready to sacrifice
her whole social group (husband, relatives, friends, depen-
dents—everybody) to achieve something that she, like Brodie,
considers necessary and good. One important theme that runs
through the novel is that of possessive love: the desire of someone to make another person over into the image of himself
or into the image of his dream of success. Another theme is
that of unrequited love. Thus *Three Loves* becomes a restatement
and commentary on some of the ideas in its predecessor, but
without the bizarre and exaggerated brutality that overshadowed
its events.

Characteristically, Cronin's title pervades his book. According
to Lucy's cousin-in-law, Anna Galton, the story concerns a lady
who is too possessive of her husband, her son, and her religion—

"The Father, the Son, and the Holy Ghost," Anna flippantly calls them.[18] As she warns Lucy: "You'll find out you've been chasing balloons. . . . You squeeze the balloon that hard you're going to burst it one of these days" (139–40). Those are the three loves of the title, and that is the story.

Once again, Cronin divides his novel into three parts; this time each division corresponds to one of the heroine's loves. Lucy's first love, Frank, is a lackadaisical but upright man who is genuinely fond of his wife. They have a small son, Peter, and live in Ardfillian, a suburb of Glasgow. When Frank's cousin, Anna, comes to visit, Lucy tortures herself into believing that her husband is the father of Anna's illegitimate child. Frank leaves to escort Anna back to Ireland, and Book 1 comes to a melodramatic close when Lucy's pursuing sailboat runs down and kills Frank in a heavy fog.

Now her son, Peter, becomes the object of Lucy's possessive love. Fleeing from the unwelcome advances of Joe Moore, one of Frank's brothers, Lucy takes refuge with Miss Hocking, a female lunatic who tries to strangle her. After several more adventures she settles with Peter in a Glasgow garret. There she struggles to exist so that her son may take his degree in medicine. But this situation does not suit him, and he leaves for London to be with Lucy's rich brother and his wife. The inevitable defeat for Lucy comes when Peter secretly marries. Once again, Lucy is estranged.

Lucy's last great love is for Jesus. Thrown back on herself, she experiences a religious crisis and at length is received into a convent in Belgium. Here she finds neither ecstasy nor peace, but only an intolerable demand for submission—the one thing she has never been able to offer. She leaves the convent a dying woman, to end her life unidentified in a London hospital.

This comparatively simple narrative is an appropriate method for telling a story of essentially sympathetic people caught in a dramatic, tragic situation. The loss of Lucy's three loves gives the book its unity. Her relationship with Frank, Peter, and Jesus divides the total space of the novel into thirds. With Lucy's retirement to the hospital, the author completes the structural design.

A person can destroy what she loves too much, and in *Three Loves* we are made to feel that the heroine's doom is inevitable.

From the beginning Cronin creates tragic expectations, and these conditions influence our response throughout the novel. Because he lets us know from the outset what the general course of the story is to be, he gives up the element of surprise and depends, instead, on his management of catastrophe, pity, and terror to maintain our interest. Lucy's fierce possessiveness always causes her to lose what she is gripping: from the beginning when her jealousy first drives her husband to another woman and then causes his death, until the end, when, catching at Jesus as all she has left, she enters a nunnery and takes her last fatal step.

Although Lucy is responsible for her own fall, she is not merely wrongheaded; she would not fall were it not for ill luck. Even on the simplest level of the novel, forces are at work over which she has no knowledge or control. Her jealousy, for example, is not altogether causeless. It springs from a chain of unfortunate circumstances: Anna's arrival, the innocent friendship between Anna and Frank, discovery of the photograph of the child, and so forth. The accident by which, in trying to overtake her husband for a last appeal, she loses him eternally, is a fine piece of tragic fate. In a novel where chance events seem to play such an important part, Cronin creates a character with a fixed nature to whom the same kind of thing happens repeatedly. Chance events are catalysts that bring about the inevitable.

The characters in *Three Loves* appear substantially more like real people than those in *Hatter's Castle*. Lucy reveals before her tragic end many contradictions of character that make her far more interesting, and believable, than the uncomplicated James Brodie. Although Cronin gives her the ending she deserves, we cannot help but feel some sympathy for her; and in a peculiar way, we like her. We are sad to see her die without friends or family. Our lingering sympathy for her results from several elements in the novel.

First, she is human in her affections and dislikes and obviously vulnerable to the disappointments of life. While it appears at first that she may become one of Cronin's typical figures of tyranny and hypocrisy, that she is capable of love, even though it is tragically possessive love, distinguishes her from Brodie and Cronin's other lonely protagonists. Our feelings go out to her in her fall because she herself feels the disasters so bitterly: Frank's death, Joe's advances, Peter's exile, Hocking's attack. Along with all of this, we admire her strong will. Like so many of Cronin's heroes, she never gives up on what she believes to be the right course. She never compromises. Left penniless after Frank's death, she refuses help from Joe and sets out to make her own way. For a time she carries on Frank's business with success. Most of Book 2 relates her struggles, sometimes desperate, to keep Peter in school and see him through the university. She tolerates a wretched existence in a Glasgow garret so that her son can take his degree in medicine. All of this is profoundly moving. The persons with whom she has contact—her lazy husband, her independent-minded son, the coolly provocative Anna, the boisterous publican Joe Moore, the paunchy canon, the lunatic Miss Hocking, and the selfish brother, Richard—are rendered with sufficient solidity to make her combativeness real. As one reviewer wrote for the *New York Herald-Tribune:* "There is something amazingly like triumph in her defeat."[19]

A third and deeper reason for our lingering sympathies arises out of the very method of narration, described above. We feel pity because the heroine has fallen and terror because she is like ourselves. Her misfortunes could be ours. There is a Lucy Moore in most of us, a capacity for pride and its consequence. This pride is not only pride of place or position or wealth, but pride of the intellect: the beguilingly insidious idea that we know more than others and are somehow wiser and better than they are. Other people should automatically admire us, and our inner lives should likewise be a kind of pleasing drama. Frank identifies this quality in his wife when he says to her, "Your own way. Your own way. And nothing but your own way" (42). We might go further and say that some form of deception is the basis for all of Cronin's work. *Three Loves* consists of irony, the deception of the hero. It is the story of Faust—albeit a rather sorry one—who aspires to take charge, shape other people's destinies, become "a most notable success" (45). In pursuit of this success Lucy becomes prideful, alienates herself from her simple, sturdy husband, becomes contemptuous of her cousin-in-law, and then accidentally kills her husband. From there her terrible fall continues.

In spite of Cronin's searching exploration of theme and careful planning, however, Lucy's story suffers from some of the same weaknesses found in *Hatter's Castle*. A major obstacle to the novel's total success is Lucy herself. Although we follow her closely for 592 pages, we know only that she is determined, possessive, and overconfident. She is given exactly the kind of strength and weakness necessary to her suicidal story, but nothing more. Cronin does not explain adequately her motivation. Also, some of the minor characters are even less realized: the husband who is simply weak, the son who is simply selfish, and the other characters who are simply there.

Also contributing to the novel's weakness is that Books 2 and 3 are overladen with incidents that appear to add little to the development of the central theme. In places Cronin finds circumstantial details a useful substitute for characterization. He gives us too many details relating to Lucy's possessiveness of Peter, too many specimens of Hocking's lunacy. Lucy's ride with her son and its aftermath are recounted at too great a length. Joe's advances on Lucy seem needlessly detailed. And we may question whether Cronin's lengthy commentary on the convent, effective though it is as satire, does not weaken the novel.

Three Loves suffers, therefore, from being a rather loosely constructed novel rather than one that is tightly knit and unified by elimination of extraneous material. One reviewer's comments seem particularly appropriate here: "What it needs more than anything else is a judicious editorial blue pencil. Dr. Cronin suffers from the excellent fault of too much energy, too many things to say, too much support of his central theme."[20]

In conclusion, the final lingering note of both *Hatter's Castle* and *Three Loves* is one of despair arising from the contemplation of a world filled with pain and loss. So emphatic is this note that it drowns out the conventional notion of the value of suffering and defeat. This is not so in his next novel, *Grand Canary*. Although it seems to have been planned as a continuation of the two previous books and opens with a sober account of yet another obsessed human being, the work differs markedly, in both theme and technique, from both *Hatter's Castle* and *Three Loves*.

Grand Canary

Both *Hatter's Castle* and *Three Loves* are somber, tragic books—
what one reviewer described as "grim masterpieces."[21] His third
novel is different. Although we find in it both tragedy and melodrama, it does not affect us as an oppressive book. Rather, Cronin
gives us a blend of fact and fantasy, a happy ending of redemption, humor, and a lightness in the exotic settings of the sea
and the Canary Islands not associated with the mists of Scotland,
which enveloped the earlier books. Above all, in his new novel
Cronin stills those critics who complained that he lacked "spiritual gifts," that he suffered from "inaccessibility to a spiritual idea."[22] Not only is *Grand Canary* based on a "spiritual
idea"—selfless dedication to truth seeking—but it permits its
chief character to realize his "spiritual" ambitions, to tran-
scend the strain and the sordid struggle that had defeated the
earlier characters.

To develop the plot, Cronin draws from a convention that
has become familiar in a long line of successful books and motion
pictures since Vicki Baum's *Grand Hotel* (1930). W. Somerset
Maugham, Rudyard Kipling, Crosbie Garstin, Jack London, and
many other writers have worked in one manner or another
with similar plots: that of isolating a group of characters, as
incongruous as possible, in a boat, train, hotel, or the like, and
showing how they react upon and influence each other. In his
use of a ship as an emblem of an isolated society, Cronin may
well have been influenced by Robert Louis Stevenson's *The
Ebb-Tide* (1894). Also Cronin's own experiences on shipboard,
many weeks confined with the same company, the flux and the
terrors of the sea, the landfalls of islands that were themselves
isolated and vulnerable societies, must have been another influence.

To this narrative Cronin has added, most seriously, a conversion theme. Like the familiar conversion of the great Victorian
novel, Harvey Leith turns from self-regard to love and social
responsibility. He is transformed by seeing and understanding
his defect and its origins, in a way that neither James Brodie
nor Lucy Moore ever could.

The plot is, as usual, slight and straightforward, its basic outline almost sentimentally trite. It shares with its predecessors

the scheme of having one central figure who is ruled, at least temporarily, by an overpowering obsession. In this instance, the character is Harvey Leith, one of Cronin's idealistic doctor heroes fighting for his own kind of integrity. The dominating force is his cynical scorn of a professional world that has blamed him unjustly for the deaths of three patients. Plunged into almost sudden alcoholism in his search for oblivion, he submits to the advice of his friend, Gerald Ismay, who ships him off on a voyage to the Canary Isles in hope of mending his shattered nerves.

On board the *Aureola* the doctor meets seven other characters: Jimmy Corcoran, a broken-down pugilist who visits wherever he might see the chance of picking up a shilling; Robert Tranter and his devoted sister, Susan, two ardent missionaries and the only Americans in the drama; Mother Hemmingway, who operates in Santa Cruz an establishment of ill-repute; and Lady Mary Fielding with her two travel companions, Daines-Dibdin and Elissa Baynham.

Although all seven characters contribute in some way to Leith's regeneration, it is through Lady Mary Fielding, a wealthy young matron, that Leith learns how potentially destructive emotions can become inspirational. This change of character occurs after he nurses her through a severe attack of yellow fever. He saves her life at last by a transfusion of blood from his own body. Because of his love for the lady, he comes alive for the first time to others, particularly women, but to himself as well, understanding as he never had before his own resources and needs. He loses his coldly scientific attitude and develops a serious sympathy for human suffering. When Sir Michael Fielding flies down for his wife and insists that Leith return with them for a triumphant visit at their luxurious estate, Leith gets a new job and Lady Mary as well.

The literary effectiveness of the story depends in part upon Cronin's irrepressible power to tell a gripping story. For one thing, *Grand Canary* is noticeably concise when compared with its forerunners. In studying the structure of the novel we are likely to notice first how carefully he links the chapters. The first words of a chapter usually tell us where we are in the narrative and what is coming next. A few opening statements, chosen at random, will substantiate this point:

The ship, too, seemed waiting. (Chapter 2)

Just after seven bells on that same day Harvey Leith came out of his cabin for the first time since the ship had reached blue water. (Chapter 8)

Two days before, when the *Aureola* pounded out of Orotava Bay, Mary Fielding watched her go. (Chapter 18)

Afternoon of the same day. (Chapter 21)

The following evening; and dinner was over. (Chapter 29)

Thus we are led on through the book rather in the way a seventeenth-century French dramatist kept the action running smoothly by *la liaison des scènes*. No characters leave the stage until the next group has emerged from the wings and is ready to speak.

Though the novel is not presented as a journal of the cruise, Cronin also lets us know exactly where the *Aureola* is at each stage of her voyage from England to Santa Cruz, again using the opening words of many of the chapters to give the clue. These navigational notes do not always relate to the substance of the chapter. Cronin puts them in, perhaps, because he wishes his book to appeal to readers of voyage literature who want the facts about wind and weather, longitude and latitude: "The ship was slapping into the Irish Sea" (Chapter 5); "They were three days out" (Chapter 7); "On Saturday they made Las Palmas" (Chapter 9). By this device Cronin simulates a voyage.

There are six kinds of chapters, all nicely fitted together. About one-fifth of the novel reports the routine of life on board a banana boat: sleeping, eating, killing time. But Cronin is writing a work of fiction, not a treatise or an autobiography. Consequently, he devises a number of chapters to provide his narrative with peaks of suspense and excitement. There are eleven of them, fairly evenly distributed throughout the book.

Although there is no towering character like James Brodie, the impression these sharply delineated characters and incidents leave is a lasting, if sometimes unpleasant, one. Since all thirty chapters are built around a single character or group of characters, we can see that Cronin uses such chapters deliberately as a device in constructing his narrative. He does not introduce these men and women aimlessly. In every instance he uses their words and actions not only to entertain but to make a point. The characters both tie the episodes together and run like a thread through the book. They also suggest the alienation that the hero suffers, then his growing sense of self-identity and self-sufficiency, and finally his rebirth. The following passage reveals Cronin's narrative method:

So they set out to keep moving, steering a course through the wet streets, encompassed by a hurrying stream of elbowing clerks and typists, trudging past opening shops and cafés and offices and squat bounding taxis which invited them in vain. Beside Ismay's short, well-groomed form, clothed with the dapper opulence of the successful man, Leith's striding figure struck an arresting, almost painful contrast. He was tall, badly dressed, and spare, with an angular leanness which gave his movements a queer abruptness. His face was very pale, unshaven, the features set to a fine edge as though chiselled. In the fixed harshness of his expression openly displayed there was something burning. It was like a burning contempt of life—bitter, scornful, austere. And yet his wide, dark eyes betrayed him. They were wounded eyes with far-down glinting depths in which a sensitive comprehension lurked and quivered.[23]

Here the narration and description characterize the style of the novel as a whole. Cronin first sets the scene; then he describes the characters (facial description and dress reveal general personality; description of the eyes reveals the hidden meaning of the character); he finally allows them to talk out the problem, while making interlineating comments about the meaning of it all. We learn about the characters from what we see and from what we are told. Many of the adjectives in this passage, as well as in the novel as a whole, are tags or labels for characters.

Leith's regeneration is one portion of a wide-ranging concern in *Grand Canary* about how destructive emotions can become inspirational. But his gradual expansion into a loving, humane man also functions as a kind of organizational principle, uniting the common interest of a variety of disparate characters. Religion, for example, receives a skeptical treatment. Robert Tranter, a Seventh-Day Adventist missionary from Trenton, New Jersey, is Cronin's equivalent for Maugham's Dr. Davidson in

Rain (1917). Both men have the gift of gab, are emotional in their religion, and view their future charges, the natives, with contempt. Unlike Davidson, however, Robert is neither taciturn nor morose, but a great smiler, handshaker, and personality-pusher. In his crude, brash manner he tells his sister:

Personality counts in business anywhere. Good enough. I'll say it counts double in the biggest business deal in life. And that, Sue, is putting over the Word of God. (87)

Also reminiscent of the Protestant missionary in *Rain,* Robert is an interfering busybody who considers his own superficial and compromising religion superior to the ancient and satisfying faith of so-called primitive peoples. He is humorless and a killjoy. He abhors smoking or drinking, but is addicted to women. His most disgusting characteristic is his hypocrisy. In him it takes the sanctimonious form of mixing religion with lust, and claiming that an opportunity for illicit intercourse is providential. Cronin's verdict on him is probably that expressed by Elissa Baynham:

You're all surface, my saintly friend, and quite hollow inside. You're not a man. You're a fool, a selfish Bible-banging fool without the backbone of a spider. I'm selfish and know it. But you—you're the most hide-bound egoist that ever hummed a psalm tune. And you think you're a God-sent minister of the Light—Heaven's gift to humanity. You say you're sincere. That's the worst of it. If you were a hypocrite, I might respect you. But you believe you're a saviour. You bound about, roaring salvation. And how you like it. Then the moment you're hurt you start to snivel. (236)

Together with structure and characterization, Cronin also turns to myth and symbolic action to unify his novel. Clearly, the construction of the story follows in detail the traditional formula of the quest. Cronin's main theme is the discovery of the self. The progressive movement of the hero is that of separation, initiation, and return. Within this general framework Cronin plots his story with individual variation.

Certainly Leith is most in need of some kind of renewal. He boards the ship "charged with that searing bitterness which, like an acid, had consumed him, drunk or sober, for the past three weeks" (5). The first sight of his cabin bunk—"white as a shroud and narrow" (11-12)—reminds him of the coffins bearing his three patients. The sound of the waves—"hollow and sepulchral" (12)—recalls "all the ghastly panoply of death to the grave" (12). He wants to forget the past, but "the most irrelevant and trivial distractions drew him back inevitably— painfully" (8). Up to the time the story opens Leith's life has been devoted to medical research. His ignorance of love and the beauty of life is matched by his total insulation from it—a condition managed deftly by his mother (whose desertion of him as a child gave him a precocious contempt for women); by his father (who was an academic and professional failure); and later by his aunt, "a nagging and impoverished spinster" (44), who raised him after his father's death. Feeling that it is best to live a life "governed by known laws, inflexible" (96), Leith channels his energy into a medical career, grateful for the absorption provided by his studies. At the start of the voyage, therefore, it is reason alone that offers him any satisfaction and a means of expression.

Leith's one true friend, Gerald Ismay, represents in the novel the detachment of wisdom and the dignity of not giving in to unpleasant events. Within him lies a sensibility and intelligence that responds to his friend's needs. He believes in Leith's innocence, persuades him to take the sea voyage, and arranges with the captain that no drinks be served while he is on board. Not by accident is the *Aureola* selected for Leith. In its name is symbolized the hope Ismay expresses: "The celestial crown won by a martyr, virgin, or doctor, as victor over the world, the flesh, or the devil."[24] Ismay's confidence in himself and his friend is apparent when he tells Leith: "I know you'll do great work. I feel it. You've got it in you just—oh, just as Pasteur had. I'm positive. Don't let yourself go to pieces like this. It's too horrible" (13). When he sees Leith safely aboard ship, he turns to go, and his parting words prove to be prophetic: "It'll be good to have you back. . . . Back and ready to begin again" (4).

Ismay's commitment to Leith is clearly fueled by Cronin's own resentments against the professional medical world, which nurtured the crisis. Leith's exploitation at the hands of his colleagues provides Cronin with a paradigmatic instance of some of the injustice he detested throughout his life and protests

44 A. J. CRONIN

against most notably in *The Stars Look Down* and *The Citadel.*
From Ismay we learn that Leith's patients died not because of
his serum treatment, but because the hospital authorities had
delayed too long in permitting him to administer it. Yet in
the public's unscientific mind, and in the unscientific minds of
his relatives, Leith's serum—not the disease—killed the patients.
Retreating from the confusion and disillusionment of his past,
Leith moves toward a coherent sense of self largely through
the agency of his relationship with Lady Mary Fielding. Ironically, she, too, is seeking to escape, but from a life too soft,
from a husband too kind. If we are moved to expect anything
like the conventional outcome from their first meeting, we are
mistaken. The relationship between them, writes the reviewer
for the *New York Times Book Review,* is "a delicate, original
and moving contribution to modern literature."[25] Although they
are mutually attracted to each other from the beginning, her
gradually dissipating confusion and his reluctance to commit
himself definitely require some time to resolve themselves. On
the third day, for example, she asks him to tea on deck, and
he finds himself unwillingly yielding. In the dialogue that follows
Cronin introduces the precognition theme that will figure so
prominently in the novel:

"Don't you ever feel happy," she asked dreamily, "without knowing
why? Just without any reason?"
"There is no reason," he answered morosely. "Happiness is an
unreasonable state. Examine it and it disappears."
"You don't want to examine it," she murmured; . . . "I'm happy
now at this moment. I must tell you. I know; yet I can't actually
explain why." She spoke more slowly and very seriously, like one
groping beneath the surface for words. "It's so puzzling. The moment
I saw you I had the feeling that I knew you, that I had met you,
that you would understand. Like a memory—deep down, a long way
off." (73–74)

Accompanying these inexplicable feelings, Cronin writes, is
a recurrent vision:

a place hauntingly familiar, of a perfume lingering, elusive, of a garden,
sweet-scented and profuse, set in the shadow of a snow-capped peak,
bathed in clear moonlight, hushed by the whisper of a distant sea.

Often this garden came to her in sleep and she would run gladly
and wander there, fingering the flowers, lifting her face to the moon,
feeling a lovely inner joy which irradiated her like light. Next day
she would be sad and quiet and alone; she would feel herself odd,
strangely out of key, separated from the ordinary things of life. (41)

The moonlight, the floating mist, the nodding lilacs and labur-
nums, the weedy bottom of the sea, are summoned on stage
from the greenwood of English pastoral convention. To her
friend Elissa, to her husband, and indeed to most people with
whom she has shared this dream, she is nothing but "like a
child looking at a rainbow" (42). "You must learn to grow
up," Sir Michael tells her one day (41). But Leith is fascinated
by the story and the way she tells it: he "could not believe
that she was serious; but her gaze—so grave and so intent—
held him strangely" (75). He is suspicious of her sincerity,
moved by her tears, curious about the dream, and suddenly
"deeply within his soul there was a stirring as from a movement
of uncertain wings" (75–76). Spending only a few precious
moments together, Lady Mary and Leith nevertheless grow inex-
orably close to each other, needing only some kind of catalyst
to stimulate explicit avowals of love. The epidemic of yellow
fever at Santa Cruz provides precisely that.

The rest of the novel is almost entirely concerned with the
progress of their relationship. Moving into the primitive interior
on a journey fraught with all manner of Conradian overtones,
Leith and Lady Mary disengage themselves from the rest of
the group and find their House of the Swans and the garden
with the freesias just as she had dreamed. In the solitary intensity
of the moment Mary explains to Leith that she loves him: a
solemn declaration that he solemnly repeats. They embrace and
remain wrapped in the grip of powerful feelings neither can
really understand, feelings that open rapidly the way to a new
intimacy and honesty between them: "I have never known anything like this," he says, "nor anything so beautiful as you. I
can't understand. But I know that all my life has been nothing
up till now" (197). To rescue her from death becomes his mission. For the first time in his life he learns what it is for a
doctor to want to save a person, not only to combat the imper-
sonal course of disease.

Some of the most vivid chapters are those in which Cronin describes Leith's desperate battle and his final daring but successful experiment to save her life. We see him as both cynic—who deceived himself into believing that his destiny is fixed and realizes that he and his world are still to be explored and discovered—and rationalist, who realizes that reason alone is insufficient for his quest. The experience at Sussex Mansion ultimately serves to impress upon him what the narrative so forcefully impresses upon us. Leith finds little comfort in self-reliance. As another lonely, embittered man in search of a human shoulder, he succeeds in such a quest. Lady Mary's love "redeems" his heart:

His whole attitude towards life was swept and shattered; and from the ruins had emerged this shining revelation. No longer could he find a jibe with which to mock the weakness of humanity; no longer was he cold and hard, contemptuous of life. Life now seemed rare: a lovely, precious gift, fraught with strange, unconsidered sweetness. (254)

We see, then, that Harvey Leith is the opposite of James Brodie. To save a stranger he risks his life; Brodie would not pause to help a neighbor. To defend Jimmy Corcoran he involves himself in a fistfight; Brodie attacks Denis Foyle and Mary out of pride. Finally, Leith shares in a recognition of God, but Brodie only harangues the possibility of one. Leith finds values hidden to Brodie because he shares common duties, common dangers, and common feelings. He subordinates his ego to assist his fellow human beings.

Another reason for the novel's difference is that it brings almost entirely new subject matter into Cronin's fictional world. There had been doctors in Cronin's earlier novels, but Harvey Leith, once he is on his way, is not primarily a doctor but a research scientist fighting for his different kind of integrity. He is a new hero, scientific idealism a new subject, and scientific individualism a new (and rather unscientific) perspective.

This new subject matter exists, however, within a familiar Cronin pattern: the young person who has his glimpse of values beyond the reach of his environment (in this case, beyond the reach even of the professional environment), his struggle to achieve his vision, his success after sacrifice. But the variations in the pattern make this novel seem almost to present a new Cronin: Leith *is* a hero, as earlier central figures are not. The hero, after his fumbling, acts on a platform of clearly defined affirmation. The hero can both love and give up love. The woman whom the hero loves is also a heroine, one whom contemporary readers can themselves love and admire. Lady Mary seems to be a "realized" character, unlike the women in the earlier fiction.

Finally, the literary effectiveness of the story depends also upon its exotic setting and the pervading suspense entailed in its hero's more and more anxious determination to save Lady Mary's life. But even without this suspense *Grand Canary* would be a remarkably interesting book. The freshness of its description, far more vivid than that of the ordinary travel book, is apparent now as it must have been to Cronin's first readers. Beautifully written, with language verging on the poetic, *Grand Canary* is, of these three, Cronin's best book.

Although we do not experience the usual passion of the crusading reformer to be found in the later books, *Grand Canary* does constitute a damaging commentary on life's crude realities and betrays Cronin's growing concern for social reform and his recognition of the alarming disparity between man's profession of belief and his true attitude. Without the growing sense of desperation that slowly assumes domination of both narrative and reader throughout the latter half of the story, this charming romance might not have become the literary success and bestseller that it proved to be in 1933.

Conclusion

Cronin's first three novels constitute his literary apprenticeship. In them he sees his characters and locale through a haze of either melodrama or romance, yet at the same time we can detect unmistakable signs of those qualities of mind and art that are to stamp the later mature novels with their author's particular originality. All three novels are much more than highly readable potboilers, peopled with engaging and memorable characters—though they are that, of course. Like Emily Brontë, Charles Dickens, and Thomas Hardy—three writers

with whom he is often compared—Cronin is a born storyteller
who transcends the category of "academic" fiction-writer. In
all three novels, though most effectively in *Grand Canary,* he
is able to sustain an entertaining narrative momentum without
sacrificing attention to the demands of the rigorous craft of
writing. Traditional materials become their very fabric. First,
the novels purport to present the experiences of actual people.
Second, they present life not in the vacuum of timelessness,
but in the very timely flux of ordinary experience. Third, they
rely on a very rapid mastery of the different settings and environments to which Cronin's travels had taken him. Fourth, the
prose style eschews eloquence for eloquence's sake and adapts
instead an antiliterary landscape so as to reflect better the ordi-
nariness of ordinary life.

Despite the occasional uncertainty and even crudeness with
which themes and techniques are handled, these novels also
provide an invaluable, if limited insight into Cronin's habit of
mind. They contain most of those preoccupations that we associate with his mature work. First, they contain character types,
satirical passages, situations, and themes that foreshadow his
later novels. As long-suffering women, for example, Margaret
Brodie and Lucy Moore are ancestors of Martha Fenwick (in
The Stars Look Down), Christine Manson (in *The Citadel*), and
others. Harvey Leith is in some ways an older Andrew Manson
or Robert Shannon (in *The Green Years* and *Shannon's Way*).
The desire for escape from a stultifying environment that charac-
terizes each of the early books also recurs in the later ones,
although the tone grows much harsher and the escape becomes
a rejection of an entire part of the social system.

Each of the novels also has a number of satirical passages,
with the satire usually directed at characters rather than institutions—a greedy, self-centered physician; a lunatic; a group of
jealous scientists. But because the satire is scattered and without
a frame of reference, it generally lacks the corrosiveness of the
later Cronin. Only in those works do we see the realist, social
critic, keen-eyed observer of his civilization's sins.

Throughout his writing, Cronin displays his belief that happiness is not attainable by the individual in isolation, but may
be found in shared experience. The man or woman whose isolation is self-imposed through repudiation of his social ties creates

sorrow for himself and pain for others. The person whose solitude is thrust upon him is to be deeply pitied. In his criticism of the voluntary "isolato"—the man who would forsake the common continent of humanity to maroon himself on his own island—Cronin may conceivably have had in mind John Donne's memorable metaphor: "No man is an island, entire of itself; every man is a piece of the continent, a part of the main."

Finally, in these books we see not only Cronin the romantic but a Cronin willing, unfortunately, to use his talent as a commodity. Part of the truth, certainly, is that they were written for a market and for the money Cronin needed, first to leave the medical field, then to write full-time. He had already decided that he could do slick work to support his serious work, and the publication of such dissimilar books as *Hatter's Castle* and *Grand Canary* seems to bear him out.

But in his next novel Cronin relinquishes the attempt to write for the readers of slick magazines, to write instead for himself out of his own life about things he knew and believed. Perhaps personal qualities—of honesty and goodness—dictated this change. Perhaps it was not a matter of conscious choice. Whatever the motive, the choice was not only the right one in the literary sense that it led to better work than he had done before, but also, somewhat surprisingly, in a commercial sense. The first novel of Cronin's best phase is *The Stars Look Down*.

Chapter Three

In a Mousetrap

Now fully committed to the novel, Cronin began a fourth immediately upon finishing *Grand Canary* in 1933. When he finally sent the manuscript to his publisher two years later, he did so frankly in the hope that its 250,000 words would surpass any of his earlier novels. Many reviewers of the published novel believed that it did. To the *Irish Times* it was Cronin's best novel yet: "wider in scope, deeper in human sympathy, and greater in the totality of its achievement."[1] The *New York News* praised Cronin for his "surer pen" and "more penetrating eye."[2] Hugh Massingham, writing for the *Observer,* felt that "Dr. Cronin has succeeded in the real business of the novelist, which is to illuminate society by the interpretation of human lives."[3] The *New York Times Book Review* found him to be "uncannily like Dickens" and listed the work among the best novels of the year.[4] The *San Francisco Chronicle* predicted that the novel would find a wide and enthusiastic audience, "both because it is a story and because it is a story with a meaning."[5] Almost all reviewers agreed that, of his early novels, Cronin's powers as a social novelist are most fully realized in the first of his big novels—*The Stars Look Down.*

Plot

The Stars Look Down is the most ambitious, the most searching, and undoubtedly the most intricate, both structurally and thematically, of all Cronin's novels. Its action ranging over much of England, the novel takes in the period from 1903 to 1933. The story's center is the Neptune coal mine in Ryneside County—an imaginary name for Northumbria. The plot moves back and forth between two families, the Fenwicks and the Barrases, adding constantly to their widening circle of acquaintances. Working primarily (although not exclusively) within the minds of his characters, Cronin maintains a tightly unified texture as he changes focus from one character to another—all this in slightly more than five hundred pages.

The story begins in 1903 with the description of a miners' strike brought about by conditions the workmen could no longer ignore. Richard Barras, descendant of an ancient mine-owning family, knows what his workmen have to endure. He knows the shafts, both old and new, but he ignores the imminent dangers and goes on driving his men to pick coal out of veins that encroach upon older veins. Behind them threatens the sea. A powerful wall of water might break through at any time, and he is aware of that. He also knows that his refusal to arbitrate the strike has cost him a $100,000 contract. But he moves on, willfully blind, willfully unaware.

David Fenwick is the son of the strike leader. He wants to get out of the mines and make something of himself. He goes to school with that objective in mind. A large part of the story is devoted to his rise from hewer to Labour M.P. He meets a former friend, Joe Gowlan, in Tynecastle, and is introduced to Jenny Sunley, whom he marries. Immediately after his marriage the Neptune mine is flooded and 105 men are killed—among them, David's father. But he refuses to become embittered. Rather, he dedicates himself to the task of bettering the conditions for the miners. And although Richard is vindicated for his part in the disaster, his son, Arthur, is convinced that his father could have prevented the deaths of the men. That his father is cleared of all blame in the inquiry only heightens his own desires for social justice.

When the war breaks out, David enlists. Arthur refuses to fight and is sent to jail. After the war, David is sent to Parliament. Jenny deserts him to take up a hand-to-mouth existence in London. Joe Gowlan continues to make money. Arthur takes over the mines from his bedridden father and proceeds to make conditions better for the miners. Labor troubles begin anew, and Arthur loses his mine to Joe. David is defeated in the next election for Parliament and goes back to the pits. Jenny dies in a hospital after an operation.

Profoundly affected by the misery of an unsuccessful strike and the tragedy of the subsequent mine disaster, both David and Arthur set out to improve working conditions. But at the end of the novel, thirty years later, the stars look down upon the same grim world of want and insecurity. Arthur's idealistic schemes have failed, the Labour party has come into power only to betray the miners, David has won and lost a seat in Parliament and returned to the pits, and Joe will continue to use people to raise himself to a position of power and affluence.

Structure and Characterization

Perhaps Cronin's adventure in the genres of melodrama and romance helped him to learn the mechanics of plot. *The Stars Look Down* is much more firmly constructed than either *Hatter's Castle*—in which the plot development is rather obvious and cumbersome, with blocks of narrative given alternately to the Brodie family members—or *Three Loves* and *Grand Canary,* in which the relatively simple story lines are focused throughout on the heroine and the hero. In his new novel the personalities and relationships of six people converge. Cronin accomplishes the difficult feat of advancing simultaneously, without apparent strain, on all fronts. What is more, adequate causes are established for major actions and attitudes, and conversely—to a degree that is one of Cronin's most distinguished characteristics— actions and attitudes produce logical results.

This time the six main characters are rather schematically drawn: one character is paired off with another, usually to show contrasting versions of a general type. The six major characters fall into three pairs: David Fenwick and Joe Gowlan; Laura Millington and Jenny Sunley; Arthur Barras and his father, Richard. David, Laura, and Arthur are the generally praiseworthy characters, the ones who gain the greatest share of our sympathy. The "evil" ones, or those who obstruct the good characters, are Joe, Jenny, and Richard. The good are characterized by genuineness, sincerity, and a general lack of pretense; the latter, on the other hand, continually disguise their motives and present a false appearance. One after another these characters enter the pages of the book. Strange and puzzling as many of them must be to an American reader who knows nothing of the English mining areas, almost without exception they achieve a substantial and lasting reality.

David Fenwick is the character around whom the story revolves. He is almost fanatically devoted to bettering conditions for the miners. He tries to advance himself, goes to school, takes up the cause of labor, and eventually becomes a member of Parliament. He pleads for nationalization of the mines and for a time succeeds in his efforts to improve the conditions. He makes the mistake of marrying Jenny, however, and he is crushed by the political machine run by Joe. He loses every-thing—his wife, his teaching job, his friends—and at the end, like almost everyone else in this novel, goes back into the mine pit a defeated man.

Joe Gowlan, on the other hand, is the consummate villain. When he chooses, "none could be more genial, more affable—a geniality which warmed the heart, an affability which radiated from Joe's handsome brown eyes and revealed him as a prince of good fellows."[6] But he is also arrogant, ruthless, swaggering. By every dishonest means he has worked himself up from the coal pit to the lucrative job of manufacturing munitions. He makes love to David's wife for personal advancement, then tosses her aside. He defeats David in an election with the help of money and gangsters. Indeed, Joe represents practically every phase of villainy: from petty thievery to seduction to swindling his friends.

The two young women who form the core of Arthur's and Joe's circles are Laura and Jenny. Laura is the epitome of refine-ment, frail gentility. She tries to make Joe into a gentleman. Jenny, on the other hand, is incapable of grasping David's idealis-tic plans. She cannot see beyond her etiquette book and her efforts to distinguish the "polite" from the "low." A poor, miser-able creature, she marries an immature David, makes his life wretched, and then dies in a final effort to simulate culture and politeness. She is a familiar type: the little bourgeoise who wants to be a lady.

Arthur Barras and his father, Richard—our third pair—differ in many ways. Arthur is a gentle, idealistic man who longs for ownership of the mines so that he can make them safe, pay a decent wage, and in other ways be a humanitarian as well as a businessman. But he ends up a drunkard. He arouses not gratitude but suspicion, and thus his ineffectual personality and the hopelessness of the cause are against him. From a conscien-tious objector during the war he becomes a helpless executive when he tries to battle the depression following the war. Richard

Barras, the coal mine owner, is like James Brodie: cold, heartless, and driving. He is the conventional owner who will not listen to reason and repair the damaged property. He defends his actions even after the mines cave in and drown the men. However, whereas Brodie was crude and wanted respect, Barras is, in spite of everything, still a respected man in the community.

Clearly one of the goals Cronin set for himself in this novel was to bring his readers to a better understanding and appreciation of the miner's life. While characterization in depth is never his forte, enough of the characters are so well drawn that they are not speedily forgotten. The workers are exploited and so underpaid that the ordinary occupational diseases of their lives are aggravated by malnutrition; the daily lives of the wives and mothers are haunted by debt. In addition, bad housing conditions, overcrowding, and lack of any sort of amenities leave drink and sex as the only possible diversions. This situation is stated bluntly by the narrative voice:

each man in this vast hurrying stream of life was living for his own interest, for his own satisfaction, for his own welfare, for himself. Each man was conscious only of himself, and the lives of other men stood merely as adjuncts of his own existence—they did not matter, it was he who mattered, he, the man himself. The lives of all others mattered only in so far as they affected the man's own happiness, and the man would sacrifice the happiness and the lives of other men, cheat, swindle, exterminate and annihilate, for the sake of his own welfare, his own interest, for the sake of himself. (472)

Against this timeless ebb and flow man's petty pace seems of little importance. If the six main characters have obvious symbolic import, so has the title of the novel. Subject to their own laws and compulsions, heeding little outside them, the stars look down upon a scene of chaos and social revolution. "Did you ever look at the stars?" asks the fat man in Robert Louis Stevenson's *The Merry Men* (1887). " 'When a great battle has been lost or a dear friend is dead, when we are hipped or in high spirits, there they are, unweariedly shining overhead.' 'I see,' answered Will. 'We are in a mousetrap.' "[7] This is the idea Cronin suggests in the title and acts out through his characters. Conveyed here is something of the aloofness of eternity compared to the chaos of the earth below.

Another consideration is that more important than the individual characters is the portrayal through their lives of their region and their times. Cronin's basic strategy is to create characters who embody recognizable characteristics of people of a particular region living at a given time, and who by their interaction carry the developmental theme along. Thus the problems of the miners constitute only half of the thematic material of the novel. Cronin also presents with equal thoroughness and power that aspect of human attitude and activity in wartime—the World War of 1914–18—which came to be known as profiteering. The figure of Joe Gowlan—who rises from his place beside David Fenwick in the mines to a position of wealth and material power and at last robs David of his seat in Parliament—might seem incredible to those of us who lack acquaintance with what happened in America as well as in England during World War I. But it is all too real. It must have made bitterly significant reading in England in 1941. It did in America. These two aspects of English social history will be handled with the same broadness of vision and patient accumulation of detail in his next novel, *The Citadel,* but with an evidently greater expression of positive emotion on Cronin's part behind the individual characters.

In this work, as in its predecessors, Cronin both tells a story and exposes a situation. The two aims are closely linked, and the result is a much better plot than either *Hatter's Castle* or *Grand Canary* possesses. The analysis of the British mining industry is just as interesting as the analysis of a family in Levenford or an epidemic in the Canary Isles. The conflict in which David Fenwick is engaged, however, is far more gripping than the difficulties of either James Brodie or Harvey Leith. The story gains enormously by having a central character who is clearly sympathetic to the author, instead of only doubtfully so. We can assume the normalcy of his point of view and weep, laugh, or deplore with him when he encounters examples of irrational or vicious behavior.

Artistry

The Stars Look Down shares with most of Cronin's later fiction a firm basis in actuality: while his fiction *is* fiction, it often starts from, and in some cases stays very close to, a fact or series of facts. The central inspiration behind this novel was of course Cronin's own personal experience and scholarly investigation. The story of the hardness of the miners' lot and the injustice in the system of private ownership and control of mineral resources is too well known for repetition. An amazing menagerie of characters moves through these pages—old and young, skillful and ignorant, predatory and idealistic. No doubt all of them are real, and Cronin's criticism of this profession is fully documented and accurate in all its details. As we have seen already, he immerses himself completely in the book he is writing. In part it is this intensity that insures validity.

To depict reality, to reveal the truth with the precision of a surgeon, is the way of the naturalist writer. Cronin carried out his extensive documentation for *The Stars Look Down* in a methodical manner: several volumes of notes included conversations, impressions, and reactions. In addition, he read countless books on economics and labor. He spent a year in the mining towns of the Rhondda and Tredegar Valleys, and in 1924 secured an appointment as medical inspector of mines, which took him all over England. He took on-the-spot notes; studied mining techniques; interviewed workers and their families, directors, and engineers. As he reported in two scholarly treatises and later re-created in his fiction, he found life in these dreary, monotonous towns to be oppressive. Conditions in some of the pits, those airless underground regions, paved the way for occupational diseases: black lung disease, emphysema, tuberculosis, chronic asthma, anemia—and starvation. Hazards associated with the coal mining industry were likewise documented: death in the pit from asphyxiation, drowning, or cave-ins were not the exception but the rule. Cronin empathized with the workers. Their plight recalled, with a sense of profound anguish, the years of poverty he had known. Aided by his powerful imagination, which is essentially visual and epic, Cronin welded all the details into an artistic whole.

Much of the air of unglamorous truth comes from certain peculiarities in Cronin's style. He conveys the atmosphere of a typical mining community by piling up factual detail upon factual detail in an attempt to re-create the very look, texture, and smell of the life of the miner. Frequently, he uses the slangy, ungrammatical language of these people even in descriptive or explanatory passages when the omniscient narrator is speaking. Also, a work on a subject as technical as coal mining is bound to have a somewhat specialized vocabulary. A reader without firsthand knowledge of life in the pits must search for the meanings of such words as *collier, hewer, getter, slips, breaker, pickman,* and *pikeman.* To come to grips with the actualities of life in the mine, Cronin describes scenes such as the gaunt, unfriendly landscape, perpetually shrouded in grit; the silent and laconic manners of the miners; the pervasive atmosphere of grim suffering and endurance. The town's very name—"Sleescale," suggesting "sleazy"—is emblematic. This, then, is the backdrop to the human drama that Cronin reconstructs—a drama about defeat and disappointment, about how people are victims of the greed and selfishness of others in power.

All of these unpleasant realities account for no small part of the book's success. The story of the mine disaster, for example, is based upon a true experience. As readers we become aware that we are six hundred feet underground, a mile from the mine shaft. We wander with the miners through dark passages. We hear the rhythmic throbbing of pumps and feel the breathing of the air from the circulating systems. Then suddenly the direction of the air changes. The walls between the old Neptune and the new Neptune mines give way, and we hear the loud roar of water as it rushes through the tunnels. Like a good scientist, Cronin gives the facts. And beneath this documentation there lies a deep pessimism. Characters drift about aimlessly, fail, or simply remain trapped in oppressive environments.

As always in the big Cronin novels, precise attention is also given to topographic detail. The epic struggle of men and women against forces greater, more powerful than they is not only told in terms of action, but frequently suggested by appropriate images and colors. The opening chapter does this with great skill. Martha Fenwick awakens to a "dark and bitter cold" morning; outside, the miners' rows stretch "dimly, row upon row." "The blackness of Sleescale town, the harbour beyond with one cold light and then the colder sea"; "the stark-outline of Neptune No. 17's headgear rising like a gallows against the pale east sky, dominating the town, the harbour and the sea" (11)—all this contains the notion of storm and struggle and, with the emphasis on black, sets the most important tone of the novel, for the blackness carries with it a presentiment, a foreboding, perhaps even a prediction of disaster. Then, when the darkness is pierced by red, by the flames of braziers and the flickering of the lanterns, the feeling of terror and the notion of struggle are reinforced. If black is synonymous with gloom and disaster, the flames of this chapter are suggestive not only of conflict, but also of the hell that will be depicted in the pages to come. These details show a complete, painstaking, almost photographic realism. As with the other major novels, we can take factual accuracy for granted and proceed to evaluate this novel as artifact and vehicle for the examination of social and moral values.

Ultimately, much of the power of *The Stars Look Down* lies in its appeal to the permanent feelings and essential interests of the human race. In this story Cronin achieves a simplification of society and social relationships, and by stripping life of its inessentials he gets down to the roots of human experience. This return to the essential can hardly have been difficult for him: he was never far from it in his own life. He had little of the artificiality or the sophistication of the polite writers of his time; he habitually wrote plain English and continually reduced moral and religious problems, political issues, and economic policies to the simplest terms. His sharp dichotomy between good and bad, right and wrong, true and false, undoubtedly leads at times to oversimplification (however effectively it enabled him to make his points as a controversialist), but in *The Stars Look Down* it tends rather to clear the way for an uncomplicated vision of life lived on its simplest and most essential terms.

Conclusion

With *The Stars Look Down* Cronin achieved his first great literary triumph. Powerful, poetic, compassionate, indignant, dominated, in spite of the conflict between workers and management, by a strong sentiment of human solidarity, it consecrated Cronin's reputation. It is a massive work that approaches traditional greatness; and it surpasses its predecessors by many standards. It develops in greater depth his major preoccupations—a concern with the chaos of life, its bitterness and desolation—but keeps under restraint the tendency toward melodrama without weakening the force of his instinct for drama. Unlike *Hatter's Castle,* in this novel we do have a sympathetic hero about whom we care. Cronin shows a number of human beings engaged in an epic struggle against forces greater than themselves, a conflict in which they are doomed to defeat. The class struggle is predominant, and in the course of the novel it takes on the overwhelming quality of a cataclysm.

Yet in defeat the miners do not appear as something negligible and insignificant. They have lost a battle, but their cause is still alive. Any historical novel of worth is more than mere chronicle. Overtly and implicitly it extols or condemns—or at least brings into question—a set of values. What is extolled in *The Stars Look Down* is fortitude—heroism, if we wish—hard work, and adaptability to change. The novel is a song of admiration for a way of life that has endured, even when beaten into the earth, one that has not wavered.

Finally, the book is not without its appeal today. The depiction of the miner's life, the unfolding of a tragedy, the evocation of an environment, the compassion underlying the narrative, the obviously noble purpose of arousing the reader's sympathetic indignation to the end that some social action would ensue—all this made and still makes *The Stars Look Down* a memorable book. For Cronin, too, it is a turning point. Hereafter the combination of maturity and confidence in his writing, together with the exploration of new territories of experience, will stamp his output impressively.

Chapter Four

The Shape of Battlements

Although several earlier novels, especially *Hatter's Castle* and *The Stars Look Down,* had been critical and financial successes in England, Cronin first attracted a wide audience in the United States with *The Citadel* (1937). Reader reaction to the story made it a best-seller and produced reverberations in Hollywood. Cronin was invited to supervise the adaptation of his story for the screen, and in 1938 the novel was made into a film starring Robert Donat, Rosalind Russell, Ralph Richardson, and Rex Harrison. Forty-five years later the British Broadcasting Corporation aired a new ten-part dramatization of the novel, starring Ben Cross, which later appeared on "Masterpiece Theatre" in the United States.

Set partly in the same atmosphere as *The Stars Look Down*—the dusky, dirty towns of the English coal-mining region—Cronin's fifth novel is the savage, fiercely idealistic story of a young physician's struggle to achieve success in life. To many readers—doctors particularly—the novel's main interest lay in Cronin's indictment of both the unethical practices of the medical profession and the system under which the miners lived and worked. Using Andrew Manson as his example, Cronin tries to show that the progressive doctor is not appreciated in private practice; that the field of public health is politically corrupt; that the fashionable clinic is often a commercial enterprise; that even the best institutions of research are interested chiefly in publicity.

To other readers, the interest lay in the unmistakable similarity between the hero's personal philosophy and Cronin's own opinions. There is the same integrity of character, the same effort to focus public attention on the social forces that are responsible for many of the ills of his patients, and the same deep concern for lessening human disaster. That Manson and his creator were so popular in 1937 indicates that they satisfied similar aspirations in a large audience. In the hero, these readers welcomed the titillating sense of being "inside" the medical profession. Reading Cronin, they enjoyed the especially comforting thought that they were being educated as well as entertained.

Plot

The course of the story, as usual, unfolds in strict chronological order as effect inevitably follows cause, without conspicuous digression or flashback. Its hero, Andrew Manson, is a well-trained, intelligent, and ambitious young doctor who comes to his profession with a raw and stubborn idealism and a promise "never to take anything for granted."[1] Just out of St. Andrews University Medical School, he arrives at the mining village of Blaenelly, Wales, to assist Dr. Edward Page. There he immediately finds himself out of tune with everybody not only because of his youth and inexperience, but also because of his ethnic background (he is a Presbyterian Scot). To Manson's surprise, the doctor is partially paralyzed, but his wife insists that he is only temporarily ill and will be back to work directly. The hero soon learns that she maintains this pose to keep the doctor's name on the list and to receive all the fees from which she pays the assistant only a small stipend.

Mrs. Page is the first but not the last obstacle Manson has to handle in this ugly mining town. Ignorance, prejudice, lack of equipment, and the criminal indifference of the district medical officers also pose problems for the young doctor. Not long after his arrival, he is forced to dynamite the sewer surreptitiously to prevent a typhoid epidemic. He also contradicts the diagnosis of a superior and saves a miner from the insane asylum. Through all of his struggles he carries with him the fear of losing his job. If he is dismissed, he will not be able to pay his debt for his medical education and, with a blackened reputation, he will not be able to get another post.

One compensation for his miseries is that he meets two persons destined to have a lasting influence on him. One is the shy, bitter, but honest and competent Dr. Philip Denny. This friendship lasts throughout the novel and in the end becomes a partnership of a new kind in England. The other friend is the spirited but stable school teacher, Christine Barlow. Eventually they fall in love and marry.

Six months later, Manson leaves because he refuses to work any longer under the financial domination of Mrs. Page. He advances to a larger mining company and to a broader field of work at Aberalaw, where without a dissenting vote he becomes a member of the Medical Aid Society. With him comes his wife, Christine, who helps him to acquire two higher medical degrees. His studies also lead to original research on the problem of the physiological and chemical effect of anthracite dust on the lungs of miners.

But as was the case in his first position, he is frustrated again and again by the jealousies, indifference, and indolence of both his young assistants and his superiors, and his rage serves merely to arouse their antagonism. He becomes involved in a dispute with a lazy miner whom he has put back on the work list; with a small-minded clerk to whom he has refused to give some requested birth control information; with ignorant nurses, ignorant committeemen, venal doctors; and with the townspeople who have him tried unfairly for vivisection. Not wanting to carry on in such an atmosphere, he resigns.

Because of his thesis on lung diseases, Manson is next hired by London's Coal and Metalliferous Mines Fatigue Board. There he hopes to continue his research. But to his bitter disappointment he discovers that the board is more interested in the survey of bandages and first-aid kits in mines than in diseases of the lungs. So once again he resigns. As the novel proceeds, Manson's integrity begins to yield to a stronger, less noble impulse.

Almost penniless, he opens a small private practice on the edge of a wealthy district in London. The thought of his poverty haunts him, and repeated discouragements have dulled some of his earlier idealism. He renews his casual friendship with Doctors Hampton, Ivory, and Freedman; rejects his earlier idealism and notions of high scientific integrity; and breaks with his wife, who refuses to subscribe to their notion of success. In less than one year Manson has changed from a sincere medical pioneer to a greedy charlatan. Increasing envy of his well-to-do colleagues has undermined slowly but inevitably his perspective, his conscience.

But when Dr. Ivory reveals his utter incompetence during a serious operation and the patient dies, Manson snaps back to his original ideals. He turns upon the entire money-mad group and breaks with their materialistic philosophy forever. A particularly dramatic scene occurs toward the end, when Manson is accused of unethical conduct by both a nurse and a jealous rival. He faces the trial board and accuses the doctors of thinking of themselves rather than their patients. In defense of his research Manson points out that Pasteur was not a doctor, nor Ehrlich, nor Haffkeine, nor Metchnikoff—nor Manson's American hero, Stillman. The fault is in the competitive system that forces doctors into rivalry when they should all be united in a common effort.

Although Manson has fallen away from his ideals, just before it is too late he pulls back from the abyss of spiritual ruin. He and Christine are reunited, but her tragic death by a motor bus soon after their reunion brings about Manson's mental suffering—and the final step of his purification. In the last scene Doctors Manson, Denny, and Hope organize an ideal clinic— "Specialized Co-Operation"—and settle in the small town of Stanborough. Denny is to perform the surgery. Hope is to oversee the bacteriology. Manson himself is to handle the medicine. Each doctor will use the laboratory whenever he desires. Each doctor will use his own specialized skills to help the others.

If there is any single clue to Cronin's intention in *The Citadel,* it is in the title. This simultaneously tragic and romantic novel was first called *Manson, M.D.,* after its hero, but it was felt that the title finally chosen was a better expression of the underlying meaning of the novel. Andrew Manson is a man who in spite of great odds tries and ultimately succeeds in freeing himself from materialistic influences. The word "citadel" stands for medical competency and medical integrity—the ideals to which Manson aspires. That this symbol is central to the plot is made clear when Christine tells her husband: "Don't you remember how you used to speak of life, that it was an attack on the unknown, an assault uphill—as though you had to take some castle that you knew was there, but could not see, on the top?" (335). At the end of the novel, as Manson leaves his wife's grave, he sees in the sky before him a bank of cloud "bearing the shape of battlements" (401). We are left to assume that Manson will once more assault the battlements, and that the conquest of them will be the greatest of all achievements.

Critical Reception

Not unexpectedly, the medical profession received *The Citadel* with both derision and praise. The *Journal of the American Medical Association* called the novel an unfair "picture of medicine either in Great Britain or in the United States" and wondered what Cronin was to gain "by overemphasizing the small percentage of evil that everyone knows about."[2] This opinion was echoed by the British Medical Association, which was holding its annual session in Belfast when the book was published. Two hundred copies were sent to its members, and a furious controversy broke out. Most of the comments were critical of Cronin for bringing his profession into disrepute. The Association's president was quoted as saying: "If the charge made in the book is not a fantasy, it is mudslinging. It is best ignored because nothing can be done about it."[3]

But it was not ignored. "Allegations grave and call for an immediate investigation,"[4] said the London *Leader*. "A. J. Cronin seems to have established a *prima facie* case for a government inquiry,"[5] said a letter to the London *New Chronicle*. "Might well hasten the reorganization of the medical service of this country on scientific lines,"[6] said the *Glasgow Forward*. Even the British Ministry of Health began an inquiry into fee-splitting and established a fund to enable two thousand physicians engaged in state medicine to take postgraduate courses. One of the reviewers went so far as to say that reading the novel had "made him afraid to fall ill."[7]

About the same time, an amusing controversy broke out in the pages of the London *Daily Express* between Cronin and its drama critic. James Agate, not very wisely, criticized Cronin's attack on Harley Street. The novelist easily disposed of Agate's criticism when he wrote: "I have not attacked Harley Street, the good Harley Street; what I have attacked is the bogus Harley Street."[8] Recognizing a newsworthy brawl, the editor of the newspaper sent John Ware to interview Cronin, who said of his novel: "I have written in *The Citadel* all I feel about the medical profession, its injustices, its hide-bound unscientific stubbornness, its humbug. . . . The horrors and inequities detailed in the story I have personally witnessed. This is not an attack against individuals, but against a system."[9] When the London edition of his book came out, Cronin showed his seriousness by stating through the press that "this famous through-street," Harley Street, should be bombed "out of existence" for the benefit of medicine and mankind.[10]

With so much free publicity, it is not surprising that *The Citadel* was on the best-seller list week after week; but its fame was no mere *succès de scandale.* The reasonable critics, on the whole, treated it with respect. Frank Swinnerton declared in the London *Observer* that "it will take the town, country, and English-speaking world."[11] Mary Ross praised it unreservedly in the *New York Herald-Tribune Books:* "Both the matter of the book and the manner of its handling mark it as the work of a thoughtful and forceful writer who here achieves a new level of maturity in his second profession."[12] Dr. Mabel S. Ulrich's review in the *Saturday Review of Literature* agreed:

[What Cronin has set out to do—and has done admirably—is to] cut through the romanticism that still surrounds the medical profession, and boldly expose the potentialities of charlatanism and dishonesty inherent in a system whereby a large group of men must depend for economic security on the real or fancied suffering of others.[13]

Other critics were more cautious in their remarks. William Carlos Williams writing in the *Nation* felt impelled to label it "a crowded story clumsily but sincerely told" before offering his more guarded opinion of the book: "It isn't a great novel, not in the sense that Norman Douglas or Ford Madox Ford would speak of a great novel. But it's a good novel, though it is often ironical to speak of a 'good novel' today."[14] The *New York Times* called it "pleasing reading even if it is not, as the publishers earnestly assure us, great writing."[15] Even the least favorable review, appearing in the London *Times Literary Supplement,* began with concessions:

As a novel Dr. Cronin's book may be reckoned his best piece of work. As propaganda it is lopsided. Anyone familiar with the medical profession or with social work has met Dr. Cronin's characters here and there. True, he has given us the picture of honest doctors in great and humble positions: but not enough of them.[16]

But the highest accolade came not from a professional reviewer but from Dr. Hugh Cabot of the Mayo Clinic at Rochester, Minnesota—whose letter to the publishers was reprinted in the *Journal of the American Medical Association:*

The book appears to be so important that I should be glad to believe that it would be at the disposal of every medical student and practitioner under thirty-five in this country. It will also give pause to everyone else who feels doubtful of the soundness of our present offerings of medical service. It is a great book which may easily have a profound influence on the future of society. In regard to the similarity of situations with which Doctor Cronin is familiar and of which he writes and those in this country, I can say at once that there is no important situation which he draws, the counterpart of which cannot be found in this country and probably more frequently.[17]

In the subsequent years the aura of popular success clung to the book, and critics began to point the way to a more sensitive and balanced reading. At its most obvious, they viewed it as an attempt to prove that the profit motive and medicine do not mix. To complicate this picture, it was also seen as a novel about married love. Beyond these aims, readers believed that Cronin intended to work in a broad satire of the British medical scene.

The Citadel remains interesting forty-five years later, however, not only for what it has to say about the medical profession of the 1930s, but for what it has to say about a human being attempting to establish for himself the meaning of his own existence. In describing the plight of a character whose exuberant confidence gives him a false picture of life, and who gradually becomes aware of darkness, Cronin echoes a typical attitude of his or any age toward a universal human problem. Manson wants to be a first-rate doctor, but he also wants to make a lot of money. The ensuing conflict is new in English literature, and has a validity beyond Manson's own class, country, and epoch. As with Cronin's other novels, *The Citadel* demonstrates its author's plea for the recognition of the needs of ordinary men and women, to be understood, treated fairly and without sentimentality, to be freed from worn-out conventions. Together, these diverse elements illustrate Cronin's mature ability to work simultaneously on several levels so that the finished product exhibits a richness of texture not ordinarily found in his writing.

An Interpreter of His Times

A. Bronson Alcott once remarked, "This is a good book which is opened with expectation and closed with profit." Cronin himself could have said the same for much of *The Citadel.* A large part of the novel's impressiveness stems from the way it functions throughout on a realistic level. Having grown out of Cronin's years as a physician and his experiences in Wales and London from 1921 to 1930, *The Citadel* may be read autobiographically—but with great caution. Though it is not precisely a roman à clef, we may be sure that the greedy Mrs. Edward Page, the bitter Philip Denny, the incompetent but fashionable Doctors Ivory, Freedman, and Hampton, and a score of others had their living counterparts in Cronin's own experience.

From a full spectrum of professional men and women Cronin tells of the jealousies of the assistants and the scheming rivalries of their supervisors, of questionable medical practices, unsanitary conditions, hostile patients, rejected treatments, ephemeral successes and horrifying failures, and always the drudgery of endless plodding hackwork. Mrs. Page, for instance, is an illiterate, scheming, unscrupulous woman who keeps the assistant under her thumb or dismisses him. She reminds us of a Dickens character as she feeds Manson the poorest food while she coddles herself with steaks and rich pastries. Dr. Philip Denny, on the other hand, is a burly but shy and overly sensitive surgeon whose medical career has been almost ruined by his marriage to a woman who has tried to make a society doctor out of him. Despite his cynicism and bitterness, Denny has great capacity for love. He is devoted to Manson. In the beginning of the young doctor's career Denny more than anyone else shocks him into thinking scientifically for himself; and then after Christine's death, Denny stands by and helps Manson in the latter's painful reconstruction of his broken and apparently futureless life.

Significantly, these supporting characters remain stereotypes, since Cronin's main point is that, except for Denny, they ease through life, think and talk mostly of fees, and scheme to get ahead. The lazy among them learn little and continue to prescribe routine drugs and treatments. The ambitious think up tricks to entice rich patients, prompting them to believe they

are sick whether or not they are. These antagonists—the nonpro-
gressive, materialistic doctors—are mostly figures of straw, their
outlines only vaguely discernible through the young doctor's
self-concern. Compared to Manson's vigor and vitality, these
characters appear flat and insipid.

Another striking achievement of the book is the solid under-
layer of fact. Almost all of Cronin's books, including the poor
ones, have this foundation, giving them a satisfying density and
bulk. In *The Citadel* the details of Manson's experiences—without the use of abstruse technical terms and too many scientific
explanations—are appealing to the reader. His restoration to
life of Joe Morgan's stillborn baby; his coal-pit amputation of
a miner's arm in the perilous tunnel; his restoration to consciousness of hysterical Toppy Le Roy; and the shocking butchery
of the operation by Dr. Ivory—all of these scenes rouse the
emotions as a means of persuading the mind. With its sober
factuality, it is not difficult to understand why this novel has
been so popular in both America and Great Britain.

Although the detail with which this medical world is evoked
is altogether vivid and convincing, the author's attitude toward
it is a good deal less than completely objective. True, it is realistic
in its avoidance of fantasy and supernatural intervention, in its
adherence to the laws of commonsense probability, in its credible accumulation of mundane detail, and in the sympathetic
character of its hero. Yet Cronin makes no pretense at maintain-
ing the severe disinterest of the thoroughgoing realist. Many
of his opinions and reactions slip naturally enough into the shop-
talk of his characters, their circumstantial accounts of their projects, principles, and misadventures. But his presence is felt also
behind the narrative, and his personal judgment, either as direct
commentary or as grim irony, not infrequently obtrudes upon
the action.

The enthusiasm that Cronin feels for his own medical ideas
is revealed clearly, for instance, when he puts Manson on trial
before the medical board. We may view this scene as Cronin's
opportunity to restate through his hero the things of which
he approves and disapproves. Speaking through Manson and
the other idealists, Cronin presents these solutions to the problems in the profession: (1) compulsory graduate courses for
all practicing physicians; (2) stimulation of all physicians toward

some sort of research; (3) introduction into medical practice of the idea of a personal grouping of doctors in one building, each specializing in a single branch of medicine; (4) accessibility of X-ray equipment for all difficult diagnoses; (5) establishment of hospitals outside of the big cities, away from unclean air and city noises; (6) recognition and use of the great scientists of the world whether or not they have specific medical degrees; and (7) decent hours and decent pay for nurses.

In other scenes Cronin proposes through his hero the elimination of the following: fee-splitting between medical men; medical endorsement of bogus health foods; often unnecessary and expensive operations and injections; the practice of abortions under other names; and the deliberate employment of the "bedside manner" for the sake of extracting big fees from wealthy patients who are perfectly healthy but spoiled and pampered. By the end of the novel we are left in little doubt about Cronin's outlook, his loyalties, or the direction of his antipathies.

However, to read the novel as only an attack on contemporary mores, using a "saintly victim" for its weapon, is to do Cronin and ourselves a disservice. Its themes obviously have a much wider scope.

Disillusionments of Life

While *The Citadel* has much to say about a society that seems unwilling to allow Manson to do his best work, while it dilates upon the evil practices of other physicians, it is also an unusual love story, with Andrew and Christine Manson at the center. To the initial Manson the author has imparted his own early buoyancy: he gazes at the countryside with "fixed intensity"; the scene fills him with "a sense of power, . . . tense and vivid"; he feels "a sudden overwhelming exhilaration springing from the hope and promise of the future." (7). He also has a tender conscience and never enjoys real peace of mind while engaged in disloyalty of any kind, whether to his marriage vows or to his scientific ideals. In Blaenelly he is a doctor devoted primarily to the active task of helping the sick. In Aberalaw he continues to help the sick but is profoundly aroused by the challenge thrown at him and his research in dust inhalation. In this activity he is as much of a scientist as he is a social healer. While working

for the Coal and Metalliferous Board his attitude is almost entirely that of a truth seeker, the immediate problem of healing
the sick then being of secondary importance to him. He is therefore a memorable characterization both as a recognizable individual and as the spirit of youth.

But for Andrew Manson youthful idealism passes as he becomes a casualty of the first disillusionments of his profession,
of humanity, of himself. Before long he realizes "how his whole
orderly conception of the practice of medicine was toppling
about him" (33). When he is not fighting individual or social
enemies, he is struggling with himself. When attending to his
own personal practice in London, he becomes almost entirely
indifferent to both of his earlier interests in healing and research,
and his emphasis now overwhelmingly becomes placed on the
material gains of his practice. This change of attitude extends
to his wife. He does not include her when he mingles among
the well-dressed quacks, sirens, and bogus medicine men. As
he loses for a time his own idealism after the years of poverty
and discouragement, and as he works solely to increase profits,
he tends also to neglect his wife.

After breaking from the London moneyed group, however,
Manson returns to his old standards. The steps by which he
frees himself from the materialistic influences are definitely
marked. That very night he symbolically flings the money sack,
filled with the day's earnings, into a corner of the surgery. He
then refuses to accept the fee of a perfectly healthy though
neurotic woman whose money he had formerly accepted with
enthusiasm. He breaks with Freddie Hampton, then Frances
Lawrence, then Le Roy, the bogus manufacturer of supposedly
scientific foods. And he reunites himself with his two old idealistic friends, Denny and Hope. More important, he is reconciled
with Christine, the finest of all the idealistic forces acting upon
him. Although Manson may be a character without great complexity, in the sense of deep philosophical self-questioning or
intellectual breadth, his life story is by no means a simple romance. Like Harvey Leith of *Grand Canary,* he is a good character: honest, idealistic, forthright, ready to speak his mind. And
therein lies his literary appeal.

Christine is effectively presented as a frank, well-educated,
level-headed young woman whose instinctive enjoyment of life

is the counterpart of Manson's integrity and determination. She is another of Cronin's long-suffering women who remains true to her ideals. She knows the secret of turning hardships into fun, of forgetting irritation in laughter. The birth and loss of their only baby cements them more firmly together. Hard work and poverty do not frighten her. The passionate integrity her husband brings to his science she brings to human relations—above all to her husband. From him she refuses to accept any compromise of principle, even though this course leads them for a time to obscurity and poverty. She is strongly opposed to materialism-for-its-own-sake and its shabby, cheapening results. She fights as best she can against every influence that she thinks will hurt her husband either as a scientist or as a man. Her figure, like her husband's, is developed solidly and consistently to the very end of the novel.

Conclusion

In *The Citadel* Cronin draws directly and intensively upon his own observations and experiences as a physician to represent seriously, and at times movingly, some of the significant problems of his day. The story of the young doctor's painful rise, his period of mistaken pursuit of material success, and his final purgation and adjustment—all this brings almost entirely new subject matter into Cronin's fiction. In *Hatter's Castle* and *Grand Canary* Cronin had written about doctors who vacillated between lucrative practice and professional integrity. In *The Citadel* his hero is not primarily a doctor but a research scientist fighting for his own kind of integrity.

To one concerned with literary movements, part of the interest of the book lies in its representation of the many facets of its cultural and social milieu. It contains elements of romantic optimism, of realistic appraisal, of naturalistic pessimism. In attempting to trace in *The Citadel* the progression of his own attitudes toward life, Cronin makes a comment about human experience that strikes home frequently with compelling force. *The Citadel* is a sound, sane, and, on the whole, true book.

Chapter Five

A Figure against the Sky

As we have seen, Cronin's medical career had a profound effect on his literary work. He had seen much poverty, much sickness; he had seen the relationship between the two. Because he was a doctor, he was a trained observer and knew how often mental dissatisfaction produces physical ills. Out of his experiences and understanding of human frailties came his novel about scientists and doctors—*The Citadel*.

Almost three years went by before he found a theme that satisfied him for his next novel. When the first draft was finished, he wrote to Christopher Morley: "While simple and very moving, I think it is by far the most important thing I have ever seen, and deeply significant today."[1]

That new novel, *The Keys of the Kingdom* (1941), emphasizes with incisiveness the problems encountered when a religious man rebels against the man-made rules, limitations, and barriers that are continually thrust between human beings and their God. Its merit lies precisely in its analysis of the conflicts between kindliness, sincere faith, and human understanding on the one side, and intolerance, bigotry, and assumed piety on the other. "Men will wrangle for religion; write for it; fight for it; die for it; anything but live for it," said John Cotton.[2] In *The Keys of the Kingdom*, however, we find a man who does live for it, who spends his life as a village vicar and a foreign missionary and who faces challenges often in his strivings after God. Francis Chisholm is the medium through which Cronin presents his conception of what has been called the most difficult subject in the world—religion.

Origins

The title for this novel comes from the words of Christ to Peter—"And I will give to thee the keys of the kingdom of heaven"—and the central theme comes from Geoffrey Chaucer's famous description of the poor parson of the town, which ends, "But Christes' lore and his apostles twelve / He taught, but first he followed it himselve." Thus the keys, according to Cronin and his mouthpiece, Francis Chisholm, are one's knowledge and use of the fundamentals of tolerance, humility, charity, and kindness. Where creeds divide, deeds of love and sympathy unite.

For the inspiration behind the hero's character, however, we must go back to 1929, when Cronin visited Rome to celebrate the anniversary of a famous saint of the Church. It was a sublime spectacle. "Starkly ascetic, rigid in self-denial," he wrote, "he had ruled a great religious order and had never done a wrong thing in his life."[3] Cronin's companion at that time, an Englishman, was so carried away by the proceedings that he insisted Cronin write a book about "this classic example of saintliness."[4] But Cronin wanted to depict problems that he believed confront the Church under every name and in every age. He wanted to direct his subtle satire chiefly against the pomp that masquerades as piety and against the narrow exclusiveness that often attempts to exclude Christ from His own church. Therefore, he decided to write about "a total opposite character"[5]—a "figure against the sky," in Thomas Hardy's phrase:

Amidst the fanfare, and the sale of gauntly profiled medals, it was amusing to visualize a short, balding, human little man who had made mistakes, fallen down and picked himself up again, something of a rebel, who hadn't believed easily, a man with human weaknesses, . . . who had been kicked around a good deal by his superiors in a good many places and yet faithfully, devotedly, obscurely, had loved and served his fellow man. For him there would be no pomp, no ceremony, no canonization.[6]

But it was not until 1939, ten years later, in the midst of the instability, uncertainty, and shock of World War II, that the time seemed appropriate for such a book:

The world was swamped with hatreds, strangled by fear, crushed beneath brutality. In the face of the sweeping tides of force and greed there seemed desperate need for the forgotten virtues: liberality, tolerance, brotherly love. . . . I felt most urgently . . . that I must make a plea for simple goodness. . . . Above all, I wanted my book to be

universal, without rancor, full of the unbiased impulse which had
motivated it.[7]

Such was the inception of what became *The Keys of the Kingdom.*
With much of the world at war, and with many writers preoccu-
pied with that topic, a book with religion as its background
was most refreshing. From 1931 through 1946 each annual
best-seller list included at least one religious book, for the need
of faith intensified when the problems of the Depression melted
into the greater problems of a new war. Many novels, both
English and American, depicted the priest, sometimes a heroic
clergyman challenging his rich parishioners, sometimes an idealistic layman who accepts the way of service and sacrifice.
In 1931 Willa Cather for the first time in her long and distinguished career attracted a wide audience with *Shadows on the
Rock,* a story of Catholic values. In 1932 Lloyd Douglas's *Magnificent Obsession* came to the best-seller lists—the first in a long
series of fictionalized homilies that expounded the gospel that
the good life for an individual could be achieved through altruism and amity based on the principles of the New Testament.
Other popular religious books of the 1930s included such diverse works as the first publication of Charles Dickens's *The Life
of Our Lord,* written originally for children; Alexis Carrel's *Man
the Unknown,* a scientist's acceptance of miracles and personal
immortality; Henry C. Link's *Return to Religion,* allying modern
psychology with the Christian faith; and Sholem Asch's *The
Nazarene,* an unorthodox but inspiring novel about Christ. In
the war-torn 1940s, when the demand for Bibles was greater
than bookstore supply, three books became best-sellers: Lloyd
Douglas's *The Robe* (1943), Franz Werfel's *The Song of Bernadette*
(1942), and Cronin's *The Keys of the Kingdom (1941).*
Of course, it is not at all uncommon, in time of war, for
the thoughtful artist to look to the past for themes. Historical
material offers the artist a certain stability; it enables him to
draw parallels with his own confused and unresolved times; it
gives him the opportunity from a safe distance to make symbolic
interpretation applicable to his troubled era; and it spares him
the risk of assessing and analyzing a contemporary world scene
that tomorrow may be so drastically altered as to annul whatever
pertinent wisdom his commentary contained. When religion is

presented logically and unpretentiously, as in *The Keys of the Kingdom,* without mawkishness or condescension, it is sufficiently novel to make the reading public take notice. In this atmosphere and with these attributes Cronin's most popular novel achieved its immense success.

Plot

As critics were quick to point out, the story line of *The Keys of the Kingdom* is in some respects already familiar to readers of *The Citadel.* In that novel, we remember, a medical doctor who saw his profession as one of service to humanity became at odds with his organized colleagues who saw medicine merely as a paying career. The moral seemed to be that if a physician chose the idealistic view, he might expect to be unprosperous and neglected, or even cast out of his profession entirely. If, on the other hand, he inclined to the materialistic outlook, he might look forward to riches, fame, and honor.

In *The Keys of the Kingdom* it is not the profession of medicine, but that of the priesthood that is held up to examination. The verdict, however, is much the same as that found in *The Citadel.* The priest who serves God according to the teachings of Christ, viewing himself as the selfless shepherd and servant of man, accepting poverty, humility, and perhaps even martyrdom, is likely to be misunderstood, undervalued, and even cruelly censored by his brethren. The worldly priest, on the other hand, will win the power and the glory that the Church has to bestow. Cronin's priest, like Cronin's doctor, is an individualist with the courage to accept the guidance of his conscience rather than his self-interest. In the Church, as in the medical profession, such courage may put one at a disadvantage, often bringing disappointment and disillusionment. *The Keys of the Kingdom,* therefore, is not only an entrancing story but also an expression of personal faith.

The novel opens in 1938 with a brief chapter properly entitled "Beginning of the End." Father Francis Chisholm—pock-marked, broken in health, and gnarled in body after thirty-five years as a missionary in China—is now sixty years old and completing his first year back in a poor parish of his native Tweed-side, Scotland. His boyhood friend and fellow seminarian,

Anselm Mealey, is now a great success as bishop. For Francis, however, it seems that parish affairs are not what they might be, and the bishop's secretary indicates that retirement to a home for aged priests is planned. That night Francis thinks back to review the story that brought him to this point. Cronin uses all but the last chapter of his book for the unfolding of these recollections: "Strange Vocation," "An Unsuccessful Curate," "The China Incident," and "The Return."

Chisholm's story begins fifty-one years earlier in the small, Scottish village of Tweedside where he lives with his father (a Catholic) and mother (a Protestant). Alex Chisholm is the head man of the Tweed Fisheries Station No. 3, and the fellowship between father and son is indeed closely knit. Fishing is not only their work but their hobby, and even on Sundays after mass both men might be found slipping away secretly through the town to the river "lest they shock finer sensibilities."[8] Unlike his friend Anselm, Francis feels no call for a religious vocation. Even at ten years old he is embarrassed when a boy publicly professes his love of Jesus Christ. But when his father, and his mother indirectly, are victims of a battle between the Catholics and the Protestants, their death by drowning changes the course of Francis's life and starts the chain of events that will lead him to enter the Church.

After four miserable years with harsh relatives, the orphaned boy is rescued, like David Copperfield, by his devoted aunt, Polly Bannon. The suicide of his childhood sweetheart, Nora Bannon, finally brings about his decision to become a priest: "First his parents; and now Nora," he thought; "He could no longer ignore these testaments from above. . . . He would give himself entirely to God" (82).

After his training at the seminary of San Morales, Spain, Francis becomes assistant to a burly, rigid-minded Irishman who has lost the hearts of his parishioners and becomes jealous when his young colleague tries to win them again. His next term of service is under the ambitious Dean Fitzgerald, who is completely taken in by a faked miracle and has visions of a second Lourdes in his district. Francis is the only doubter, and the clash between his unconventional views and the serenity of his colleagues is almost too severe for reconciliation. Francis is an individualist, and individualism is viewed by his fellow theologians as a rather dangerous quality in a priest. Hence, he is regarded by his superiors as a bit unsound, an indiscreet and inveterate rebel. Throughout his life he is shunted smoothly from appointment to appointment. From his student days at Holywell to his first curacy at Slalesley; from Tynecastle to the interior town of Pai-tan in the province of Chek-kow, China, only a couple of colleagues and friends view him without disfavor and do not place obstacles in his path.

"The China Incident"—the longest and most entertaining section in the book—reveals fully Francis's abilities. Against great odds—indifference, ignorance, antagonism, scorn—the humble priest carries on his work, concerned less with the number of converts he makes than with the sincerity of their conversion and the alleviation of suffering. Among the first to become his friend in China is the rich merchant Mr. Chia, whose son he saves from death by a simple operation. Through Chia's generosity, Francis is able to realize his dreams of building a church and a school for Chinese children.

Humble, tolerant, wistful, the aging priest becomes with the years the hub of an active and useful mission. He fights famine, the plague, floods, and bandits. But pride of personal achievement is never his. To the aristocratic mother, Maria-Veronica, however, the priest is a socially inferior creature risen to power. She comes from Germany to take charge of the mission school, but eventually she breaks down and pleads for forgiveness.

In spite of his great success over a thirty-year period, Francis's superiors at home are dissatisfied with his apparent lack of persuasion. In the final sections—"The Return" and "End of the Beginning"—we learn that Francis has been replaced by two younger missionaries. An old, tired, lame, and scarred man, he returns to Scotland—where he began his search for understanding and faith—for his last appointment. Thus we pick up his story where we left off at the end of Book 1.

Although Francis has nothing spectacular to show for his many sacrifices, such accomplishments as a rehabilitation Christian village, countless families who owe their very existence to his orphanage, and the mission itself testify to the impact he has had on China. Even the worldly clerics, who have tried to move him to more conventional methods, see something in him that

78 A. J. CRONIN

baffles them. Monsignor Sleeth, who is about to oust him from his beloved parish, realizes that he is in the presence of sanctity. He tears up his unfavorable report and prays: "O Lord. . . . Let me learn something from this old man" (343). We leave Francis Chisholm as a saintly figure who is not understood. He is a failure only in the sight of superiors who want a record of more conversions. To the Chinese among whom he lived, to his friends and coworkers, he is recognized as a man of rare virtue and courage. Like St. Francis of Assisi, he is utterly simple, utterly honest, and utterly kind.

Critical Reception

Not since the publication of Erich Maria Remarque's *All Quiet on the Western Front* (1928) had there been such excitement about a book in the Little, Brown office. The excitement this time was a good deal noisier, and of course the publishers did everything they could to encourage it. For weeks before its publication the press was teased with hints of the impending novel. Announcing it as a work of art, the publishers put nearly their full emphasis on the size and sensation of the event. An early publicity release said: "We unhesitatingly announce *The Keys of the Kingdom* as the most important novel on this list and one of the most important novels of 1941."[9] Months later, this announcement proved to be prophetically true—if sales are a reliable indicator. A nationwide poll of literary critics conducted by the Book-of-the-Month Club listed *The Keys of the Kingdom* as designated leader of the ten outstanding novels of 1941 with a phenomenal record of sales at the end of its second month on the market. That same year the novel appeared in the number one position upon its first inclusion on the *New York Herald-Tribune Books* best-seller chart, which also reported that no other book had ever done that. (The nearest to it was Ernest Hemingway's *For Whom the Bell Tolls* [1940], which reached number one position the third Sunday it was on the best-seller list.)

The appearance of the novel on 21 July 1941 also represented a major turning point in Cronin's critical reputation: it expanded his audience in kind as well as number, and it changed the quality of criticism and appreciation he would receive as a writer.

Typical of the early reviews were the comments of Mary Ross, who wrote in the *New York Herald-Tribune Books:* "[it is] a more appealing and more memorable book than any the author has written heretofore."[10] The book's serious subject and the respectability of the Cronin name also recommended it to religious leaders who ordinarily regarded fiction as frivolous and inherently dangerous. W. L. Caswell, writing for *Churchman,* recommended the book to both the clergyman and the churchman who wishes "to be quite sure that he does not 'love his party more than his church, and his church more than Christianity, and his Christianity more than truth, and himself more than all.' "[11] To Frank Fitt, writing for *Christian Century,* the book was important because it "deals with that which has eternal and redemptive values for our tragic world."[12] Notes of commendation also arrived at Little, Brown from Father Maurice S. Sheehy of the Catholic University of America; the Episcopal Bishop of Massachusetts, Rt. Rev. Henry Knox Sherrill; Mazo de la Roche, author of the famous "Jalna" novels; and other clergymen and authors.[13] These favorable notices increased both the sales and the influence of the book; in fact, combined sales in Book-of-the-Month Club and Little, Brown editions passed the half-million mark soon after its publication.[14]

Although most reviewers of the novel found more to praise in the writing than to condemn, some were dissatisfied. On the adverse side, *The Keys of the Kingdom* was called at best a good story, but "misleading, melodramatic and superficial."[15] The reviewer for *Commonweal* found the hero an honest character but also "wordy and even, at times, a prig with his pointed mouthings of pious banalities."[16] Some Catholics severely criticized the novel for being theologically unsound and an unfair picture of churchmen.[17] The most direct attack was registered in *PM's Weekly,* which called it "a classic of corn, bad taste, insufferable writing and public hoodwinking,"[18] but a writer to *Churchman* hoped that "the savage attack upon the book . . . will not prejudice anyone against this great novel."[19] Indeed, it would seem, in retrospect, that there is more that is "great" than not about this novel. Since *The Keys of the Kingdom* is still the most widely read of Cronin's novels, there may well have been more than a little substance in the enthusiastic response.

The Examined Life

Father Francis Chisholm, whose long life as a priest in England and China is the substance of the story, is clearly Cronin's finest character thus far. Like most of his heroes, he is an ordinary man, sometimes weak, sometimes mistaken; but his faith and humility—alike extraordinarily profound—repeatedly lift him to moments of insight and action. It is perhaps the warm human quality of Father Francis, the genuine appeal of his personality, that gives *The Keys of the Kingdom* greater emotional power than Cronin attained in his earlier books. Although the novel lacks the immediate contemporary sociological importance of *The Stars Look Down* or *The Citadel*, it goes beyond specific social problems to consider the ultimate motives of human conduct, the nature and origin of human goodness.

Certainly another of the virtues of *The Keys of the Kingdom* is that it presents a wide range of clerical portraits, missionary and ministerial, including a sectarian "ranter," a sympathetic American Methodist medical missionary, and a variety of Catholic priests, sympathetic and unsympathetic, with a vivid profile of a missionary Mother Superior. Like the great Victorians from whose rich tradition they spring, Cronin's characters, according to his modest moral aims, are unmistakably "good" or "bad." We know as soon as we meet them that Aunt Polly, Nora Bannon, Mr. Chia, Dr. Willie Tullock, and Bishop McNabb are "good." We also can be reasonably certain that these people will endure their share of misfortune. We can find in these characters a schooling in generous humanity. Also easily recognizable are the unsympathetic characters: Bishop Mealey, Father Kezer, Mrs. Glennie, and Monsignor Sleeth. We always know where we stand with Cronin.

This contrast between the "good" and the "bad" is apparent in the comparison of Francis Chisholm and his lifelong associate, Anselm Mealey—who lacks the feeling and innate spirituality of his friend, but who uses a certain veneer and his commanding appearance to get himself elevated to the bishopric. As a child Anselm was acknowledged by the nuns as "a truly saintly boy" (19). As a seminarian he was the most popular student in the school. His name was on the prize list; he was "good at fives and racquets and all the less rough games" (65). He headed half a dozen clubs. And yet, strangely enough, he was disliked by the rector and a few odd lonely souls. As a picture of the worldly priest, Anselm is eloquent in his sermons, popular with the women of the parish, and especially assiduous in those good works that gain him the approbation of his superiors. He attracts large donations, makes many converts, and fights the outward battles of the Church. He is even willing to capitalize on a "miracle" that proves to be no miracle at all.

Francis Chisholm, on the other hand, is the dissenter, the man who is different and therefore doomed to disappointment and failure in the eyes of the world. He is awkward in manner, spontaneous rather than calculating, and has a complete disregard for convention. Quite properly, he bears the first name Francis, the apostle of Christian love and the bridegroom of Lady Poverty. He is of the same tradition as *le jongleur de Notre Dame* and Don Camillo, in his Christian simplicity, spontaneity, and utter dedication to both God and man. He is, indeed, the eccentric individualist. As his former seminary rector sees him: "You are the stray cat, Francis, who comes stalking up the aisle when everyone is yawning their head off at a dull sermon" (144).

Additional differences between Anselm and Francis become clear as the novel progresses. Unlike his associate's family, Francis's parents were poor. At their death when he was still a child he was adopted by still poorer relations. He was not a plastic, saintlike boy. Doting nuns discovered no trace of vocation in him; the less discerning of his superiors at Holywell discouraged him. We see him as a silent, doubting young student, torn by grief and rebellion as well as by a sense of his own inadequacy. One by one we see the things of this world stripped from him.

Although Francis carries a deep conviction of personal ineffectiveness, to the lovable Hamish McNabb his vocation is all too clear. From their first meeting at Holywell the red-haired Scottish priest is attracted to the clear-thinking, shy young student. He understands the boy's earnestness and values his deep humility. Most of all, he perceives in the student the great qualities necessary for a successful priestly mission: abhorrence of bigotry, recognition of goodness wherever he finds it, and eager acceptance of the essential brotherhood between Roman Catholics and persons of other faiths. He knows that Francis would be

a tower of strength to Christians in a Chinese mission field and
therefore offers him a vicariate in China. Simple in his living,
logical and direct in his reasoning, he is, as McNabb tells him
later, far from being an orthodox clergyman, but not a failure:

> You've got inquisitiveness and tenderness. You're sensible of the dis-
> tinction between thinking and doubting. You're not one of our ecclesi-
> astical milliners who must have everything stitched up in neat little
> packets—convenient for handing out. And quite the nicest thing about
> you, my dear boy, is this—you haven't got that bumptious security
> which springs from dogma rather than from faith. (142)

Suggested here in the conflict between dogma and conscience
is the memorable way in which Cronin establishes his hero as
a Christ figure. His father, head fisherman of one of the Tweed
fisheries, symbolizes the task Francis assumes when he becomes
a priest, a missionary, a fisher of men. He seems destined, from
the start, to have generous views about people and, occasionally,
to have them justified by events. The miserable interlude of
hard work and unkind treatment as a child gives him an understanding sympathy for all unhappy people, especially children.
All through his life he is dominated by the thought he expressed
as a young boy after he had stopped a crowd from breaking
up a street religious meeting: "I've had enough hating" (36).
From his parents—selfless, pious people who suffered from bigotry—he learned the tolerance he was to preach all his life.
As he reflects later, "there could be no greater happiness than
to work—much with his hands, a little with his head, but mostly
with his heart—and to live, simply, like this, close to the earth
which, to him, never seemed far from heaven" (230). After
the death of his parents and of the girl he loved, the Church
becomes to him a solace and an opportunity to serve.
    While Anselm attends to the social affairs of the Church, Fran-
cis works with the poor and lonely. While Anselm complies
with all of the Church's teachings, Francis speaks his mind. When
one of his best parishioners comes to him for spiritual guidance,
he replies, "Eat less. The gates of paradise are narrow" (210).
When Mr. Chia, without belief, offers to join the Church as
payment for his son's life, Francis gives the following unforgetta-
ble reply: "My acceptance of you would be a forgery for God"

(177). At other times, too, Francis becomes known for certain irregularities: "Atheists may not all go to hell. I know one who didn't. Hell is only for those who spit in the face of God" (215); "I can't believe that any of God's creatures will grill for all eternity because of eating a mutton chop on Friday" (215). To one parishioner, he says, "there are many religions and each has its gate to heaven" (320). To another, he comments, "Surely, sir, creed is such an accident of birth God can't set an exclusive value on it" (259). On a table he prints the words, "Toleration is the highest virtue. Humility comes next" (310). Christ-like yet human, Francis believes in tolerance rather than dogma, and he holds humility above pride and ambition. Religion is not to Father Chisholm a matter of creed, ritual, or conformity to traditional thought or conduct, but an intensely felt experience of his relation to God. Christ came into the world to provide a *living* religion, not to instigate new forms and rituals. Christianity could be the salvation of society if only people would live it and not by habit mouth creeds and inherited clichés.

On other occasions as well, Francis's actions contrast sharply with those of Anselm's. One of the dramatic moments in the novel comes when missionaries of another sect arrive in the village. Some of the recent Catholic converts think that the proper action is to drive them away. The priest greets the Protestant missionaries as friends and collaborators, however, not as rivals and enemies, thus teaching by example that bigotry and intolerance are deadly evils that must be routed and destroyed. Another time Francis gives comfort to a dying agnostic doctor who, crying that he still could not believe in God, is answered with sublime wisdom and truth that what matters is that "He believes in you" (212). With all this in mind, it is ironic that in spite of his success with the people, Francis should consider himself a failure. He sees Anselm rising fast in the hierarchy of the Church while he himself remains an insignificant tool. His frustrations stem not from envy but from a deep conviction of personal ineffectiveness. Perhaps these very conflicts within Francis contribute to his remarkable compassion and tolerance for others—the very qualities lacking in the self-assured Anselm. When Mr. Chia learns that Francis is leaving China after thirty years of missionary effort, he says, "The goodness of a religion

is best judged by the goodness of its adherents. My friend . . .
you have conquered me by example" (320). Thus the dual
strands of the narrative—Francis's and Anselm's—mesh well as
Cronin exploits one of his favorite techniques, contrast.

Through character contrast, Cronin overtly or implicitly extols
or condemns—or at least questions—a set of values. What is
extolled in Francis Chisholm is heroism, hard work, humility,
and tolerance. The other side is the constant danger to human
well-being from self-limiting bigotry, be it racial or religious.
Cronin has touched on this moral ignominy in his earlier novels.
Here it engages our full attention. There is remarkably little
preaching on the subject in this novel, but the dismal effects
of intolerance and pride are clear.

Conclusion

The sources of *The Keys of the Kingdom*'s popularity are obvious.
Now concerned with a religious theme, Cronin reveals the same
driving narrative power, the same concern with medical matters
and care of the poor, the same arresting plot, and the same
searching, if sentimentalized, humanity of feeling. He also presents a wide range of clerical portraits, breathes a liberal and
tolerant Catholicism, and tries hard to be fair to Protestantism.
Above all, he offers an intelligible and sympathetic account of
a modern missionary priest, itself a great rarity.

If there is a weakness in the novel, perhaps it is that Cronin
does not penetrate the mysteries of grace and sin, as do Graham
Greene, François Mauriac, and Georges Bernanos. His hero,
if unrewarded by the Catholic Church, has those qualities that
a humanist would recognize, without requiring a supernatural
origin for their explanation. *The Keys of the Kingdom* is, therefore,
a novel about Christians, but not a distinctively or consistently
Christian interpretation of human nature and destiny. It oscillates
between humanist and Christian perspectives.

From all this we should not infer that Cronin is attacking
organized religion. On the contrary, he is attacking the human
weakness encountered in all organizations: the inflexible bureau-
crat, the determined autocrat, the unimaginative pedant to
whom figures—number of baptisms, communions, and so
forth—are supreme. The integrity of the individual is always

uppermost in Cronin's thoughts when he is planning a book; this is the major theme of *The Keys of the Kingdom* as well as *The Citadel.* Although Francis's actions seldom bring much cheerfulness at the end, they do bring a serenity of sorts, a satisfaction at having behaved with reasonable unselfishness. We might say with Matthew Arnold that "calm's not life's crown though calm is well," but given the complications of the modern context and the tone of the modern mood, ecstasy is not appropriate. Heroism and the tragic stance seem extravagant to the contemporary reader. Given that mood, these modest moral aims are sufficiently demanding. To achieve even these—loyalty, compassion, tolerance, unselfishness—Cronin suggests, is difficult enough.

The Keys of the Kingdom represents a summit for Cronin. Everything he had done well for ten years he does even better in this book. It is not a coincidence that for his next effort he chooses to write in a different genre entirely.

Chapter Six

The Wider Life

Cronin's next two novels—*The Green Years* (1944) and *Shannon's Way* (1948)—belong together in conception, spirit, and theme: the action begun in one is concluded at the end of the other. Although both novels deal with traditional Cronin concerns, they mark another artistic departure in that the author uses as his "frame" the device of the novel of development or bildungsroman—a term often used loosely to mean any kind of initiation story or confessional life history, any story about an adolescent or young adult. But Cronin uses the term in its more restricted sense: he intends by bildungsroman a developmental novel, a semiautobiographical work that deals significantly with the mental history, self-determination, and identity of the main character. He also sees the form as essentially a realistic one, subjective but not merely confessional, a form that attempts to connect the life history of the protagonist with some larger social issues. Robert Shannon, the protagonist, encounters many guides and influences, and he must choose the true from the false. His own temperament, warped by self-distrust, spiritual uncertainty, and impatience, often makes him bring unnecessary suffering upon himself. Like most heroes of this genre, however, he finally arrives at a philosophy that is tenable in the world he sees: in *The Green Years,* a belief in the power of the human spirit to rise above conditions of the bleakest hopelessness; and in *Shannon's Way,* a recognition of the need to "live-and-let-live."

The Green Years

We first meet Robert Shannon as an eight-year-old orphan who, after the deaths of his parents from tuberculosis, must journey from Dublin to live with his maternal grandparents in Drumbuck—a small, defiantly Protestant suburb of Levenford on the Clyde. As the child of a daughter who married against her parents' wishes, Robert is accepted out of a sense of duty rather than love. Both at home and at school, he is an outcast, "barely acknowledged, poised on the edge of the unknown."[1] His name, his looks, his clothes, his upbringing, and his Catholicism are objects of ridicule in this intolerant and provincial community. From what was a warm and affectionate environment he has been transplanted to one that is cold and cheerless. Yet Robert's life in Levenford is not entirely bleak. His friendship with Gavin Blair, a naturalist, brings to him the scientific basis of his later medical studies. Jasper Reid encourages him in his desire to become a scholar. Alison Keith, a genteel and sophisticated aspiring singer, befriends him. Best of all, Robert finds comfort in his great-grandfather, Alexander "Cadger" Gow, whose goodness to the growing boy makes the story.

Gow's enormous red nose and his roving eyes mark his two weaknesses: whiskey and women. Although Robert soon comes to know him for what he is, and although he is ashamed for the old man's reputation in town, he grows close to him. Gow defends his right to Catholicism, accompanies him to attend religious instruction, and helps him prepare secretly for a scholarship examination. His ultimate desire, however, is to help Robert get what he wants most: a thorough education in biology. In this he succeeds, but only after a double tragedy that completely overturns for a time Robert's life.

When Robert fails to win the Marshall competition for a college scholarship, and when Gavin is killed in a train accident, Robert gives up his faith, his ambition, and just about everything else. In despair, he turns to Canon Roche, who helps him to rediscover his faith. When Gow dies, Robert learns that he has been willed an insurance policy, thereby giving him the chance for a medical education. Near the end of the novel Robert walks into a church—symbolizing the final stage of his initiation, and signaling the end of his "green years" and self-imposed isolation. He is eager to study medicine at Winton University—confident and happy with his newfound faith.

As the plot summary suggests, Cronin follows in part the typical narrative pattern of the Victorian bildungsroman. We can find a similar pattern—involving childhood in a provincial setting, unsatisfied education, alienation from family, "ordeal by love," the search for a vocation or a philosophy of life—in books as diverse as *David Copperfield* (1849–50), *Jude the Obscure* (1894), *Portrait of the Artist as a Young Man* (1916), and *Sons and Lovers* (1913). Each of these bildungsromane re-creates the author's own life history in some sense, but each also follows a similar fictional pattern, regardless of the particular life it reflects.

The Green Years is indeed a story of initiation, of a boy's quest for knowledge. The plot covers a period of ten years (1902–12) and falls into three sections of nearly equal length as the hero progresses from innocence to perception to purpose. In the early chapters Robert's innocence is expressed as a mixture of bewilderment and ignorance. As in Stevenson's *Kidnapped* (1886) and *Treasure Island* (1883), Cronin's novel begins with the death of the young hero's parents, and his departure from the familiar comforts and limitations of home to a section of Scotland previously unknown to him. He is an only child (Cronin himself was an only child, and perhaps as a consequence of this, very few of his characters have brothers or sisters).

The opening establishes with Proustian overtones the desolation that haunts him upon his arrival at his new home, Levenford, with his new "Mama," Grandma Leckie: "I was inclined to trust Mama, whom, until today, I had never seen before and whose worn, troubled face with faded blue eyes bore no resemblance to my mother's face" (3). At Drumbuck his heart throbs "with the dread of things unknown" (5). Standing before his great-grandfather, he feels awkward in his "ready-made, black suit, one stocking falling down, shoelaces loose, [his] face pale and tear-stained, [his] hair inescapably red" (9). Thus Robert's reactions begin in disenchantment, conveying in such pictures his sense of a hard, unromantic reality. The perceptions are Robert's, but the comic turns are Cronin's.

Robert's sensitivity to his new surroundings is apparent in his acute perception of details. At the dinner table Papa says "a long, strange grace which [he] had never heard before" (12). Robert has difficulty managing "the strange bone-handled knife and fork," does not like the cabbage, and finds the beef "terribly salty and stringy" (13). He wonders why he is "such a curiosity" to all these people and thinks, "What made them shake their heads over me?" (22). The feeling of "being watched" is an experience that is repeated and a notion that reverberates throughout the novel. Suggested here is his continual need to perform for others and to be evaluated by others. Robert is the typical uncomprehending child caught in an uncomfortable situation. Lonely, imaginative, and isolated, he lacks the understanding necessary for evaluation and perspective.

Yet *The Green Years* is not a book of simple nostalgia. Cronin has set himself the added difficulty of working within the limited consciousness of a small child while at the same time avoiding the sentimentalities of so many books about childhood written for adults. To accomplish all of this he takes his hero quite seriously, and often describes his experiences with the same gravity as Robert would view them. What is more, the novel consists of a grown man's remembered experiences, for the story is told in the retrospect of a man who looks back to a particular period of intense meaning and insight. "Our purpose," the author says, "is to reveal [the young Robert] truthfully, to expose him in all his dreams, strivings and follies" (189). This double focus—the boy who first experiences, and the man who has not forgotten—provides for the dramatic rendering of a story told by a narrator who, with his wider, adult vision, can employ the sophisticated use of irony and symbolic imagery necessary to reveal the story's meaning. Robert's unintentionally ironic comments, the other characters' laughter, and great-grandmother Leckie's overly severe and prudish reactions all point to the effect of the comic tone. The society of unpredictable relatives, each acutely concerned with his own problems, his own contradictory traits and deceits, remains apart from Robert as a boy, something he must learn in order to understand. And the narrator's tone in these early scenes reinforces the hero's innocence.

The Green Years also shows Robert's alienation by surrounding him with characters who function as negative object lessons, images of what he should avoid. Much attention is paid to the Leckie "belief system"—to their vindictive economies, their distrust of enjoyment, their preoccupation with social standing, and above all their distrust and intolerance of anyone outside the Protestant faith. Papa Leckie, for example, is a local "sanitary inspector" who in reality sees to the toilets and garbage disposal.

He is unloving, unloved, waiting only for the pay envelopes of his children. His physical description is given in terms of simple, exaggerated, eccentric characteristics:

> He was a small, rather insignificant man of forty-seven, with a narrow face, pale features and small eyes. His dark moustache was waxed out straight and his hair streaked over his scalp to conceal his baldness. His expression was marked by that faint touch of resignation seen on the faces of people who know they are conscientious and industrious yet have not been recognized or, in their own opinion, adequately rewarded by life. (13)

Mama Leckie—"the nearest to a saint" Robert has ever known (257)—is a self-sacrificing, hardworking housewife who endeavors to create a decent homelife for her family despite her miserly husband. Great-grandmother Leckie, on the other hand, is a well-meaning but ineffectual lady who lives with the family half the year and pays board to Papa. As a strict Presbyterian she tries hard to lure Robert away from the Catholic Church into which he was born.

Then there is Uncle Murdock—a weak, uncertain man who, in spite of his father's wishes that he seek employment at the Works, lives only to study plants and flowers. He fails his examinations, joins the Salvation Army, marries, and enjoys fame for his botanical projects. Later he becomes a partner in the local greenhouses and even wins a flower show award for a new carnation.

Aunt Kate, the youngest daughter, suffers from an inferiority complex because Robert's mother had been the family beauty. She teaches in a charity school that she hates, and secretly dreams of the man who will come to marry her. When love does come, Robert serves as a go-between for bowlegged, big-hearted Jamie Nigg, who works "dirty" (79) as a mechanic in the boilerworks, and Kate herself, who finally accepts him.

Certainly the most unpleasant family member is the elder son, Adam. He conceives the idea of insuring Grandpa's life. He leaves home at an early age to escape paying to Papa all that he has earned. He does well in London with an insurance company and comes home only when he wishes to borrow his father's life savings to buy a large London residence, which he intends to convert into rental units. But Adam is not a good businessman, and the house title does not clear. From him, Robert learns about "the gravities of life and the importance of money" (63). In one scene Cronin notes with irony those "natural details" of Adam's appearance. He enters the house, "confident and smiling, wearing a coat with a brown fur collar" (60). He has driven "an early Argyll model, bright red in colour, having a small brass-bound radiator stamped with the Argyll blue lion, a high wide body with handsome side seats and a door at the back" (60). While the other family members think of their shepherd pie, he sits down to "steak, cauliflower, and potatoes" (61). Later he says, "I like to get the good of my money [and] eat the best, wear the best, stop at the best hotels, have everybody running after me. That's my side of the picture" (63). Several years later the narrator looks back on this episode and says:

In my childhood I had always thought of Adam as a man who would make a fortune. He seemed earmarked for self-made success. Yet now . . . I had begun to perceive, underneath that genial confidence in himself, an odd limitation. Perhaps it was the tendency, so common in the Scot who thinks himself a "big man," to underestimate other people and their capacity to resist him. Adam was too sure that he could outwit others. (275)

Now we see that Robert's early experiences in the household expose him to a variety of characters, all of whom are caught by marked shifts in their lives: illness, the death of those close to them, the breakup of careers, and the discovery of new opportunities.

One of the obvious character-building motifs that Cronin derives from the Victorian schoolboy story is the notion that action in the world is better than passive self-indulgence. To compensate for his unhappy circumstances, Robert finds his real self by turning in part to nature and literature. His appreciation of nature, for example, may be attributed to his friend, Gavin Blair, with whom he discovers the companionship he craves. With Gavin, he hunts for a golden plover's egg in the upland marshes. Unconscious of feelings he will comprehend years later, Robert already gains from nature a sense of renewal and reassurance:

It was a new country we gained, with a breeze that came cool and
sweet as spring water on my cheek. Distantly, beneath us, lay a free
and sweeping panorama of the world laced with white roads and split
by the estuary of the Clyde, a wide bar of shimmering silver, with
tiny ships upon it. The town of Levenford was lost in a merciful haze,
out of which reached the rounded hump back of the Castle Rock.
(73–74)

Like the companions of so many of Cronin's protagonists,
Gavin is intelligent, gifted, and handsome. Particularly appealing to Robert is Gavin's "inner fibre, that spiritual substance
for which no words suitable can be found" (58). Robert's walks
with Gavin seem almost a kind of retreat to a wilderness, the
setting for meditation on the natural life he is learning from
his new friend.

While Cronin makes it clear that there is great comfort in
all this, he also shows that this friendship initiates a problem
that haunts Robert for much of the novel: a weakness for idealism. According to Cronin, the great struggle of youth coming
to maturity is a search for reality. This process involves disillusionment and pain. Robert endures a great deal of anguish each
time one of his illusions is destroyed, but these disillusionments
are necessary if he is to achieve intellectual and emotional inde-
pendence. At school he must fight with his best friend to stop
the taunts of his fellow classmates. At night he is terrified by
his grandmother's tales of Satan. He witnesses Gavin's death
and on the same day fails to win the important Marshall prize
that he so desperately wanted. All of this contributes to his
temporary loss of faith in himself and his God.

Helping to shape Robert's purpose and philosophy is Alexander Gow, the other character with whom Robert feels secure.
For the creation of Alexander, Cronin drew upon his own great-
grandfather—who had a Bergerac nose and was extremely kind
to his great-grandson when sober and "even kinder when he
was not."[2] Alexander is strongly visualized. The exterior mani-
festly proclaims the man. At his first appearance, body-shape
and costume, mannerism and gesture, all are emblematic of
his character:

He was a large-framed man, of more than average height, perhaps
about seventy, with a pink complexion and a mane of still faintly

ruddy hair flying gallantly behind his collar. . . . His beard and moustache, which curled belligerently, were of the same tinge. Though the whites of his eyes were peculiarly specked with yellow the pupils remained clear, . . . a virile and electric blue, a forget-me-not blue, conspicuous and altogether charming. (8)

This description, along with his "large, red and bulbous" nose, which Robert likens to "a ripe, enormous strawberry" (8), catches his nature: jovial, amatory, pompous. He lives on the top floor, in the only room of the house where disorder is permitted. But it is his kind of disorder, not without charm:

a strange, interesting, dreadfully untidy room. The high brass bed in the corner, with its patchwork quilt and lopsided knobs, was still unmade; the bearskin hearthrug was rumpled; the towel on the splashed mahogany washstand hung awry. My eye was caught by a black marble timepiece of the "presentation" variety lying upon its side on the littered mantelpiece with its inside in pieces beside it. I felt a queer smell of tobacco smoke and past meals, a blending of complex and intricate smells, forming, as it were, the bouquet of a room much lived-in. (7–8)

Sometimes Alexander comes downstairs for breakfast, but he takes his other meals above. His participation in family arguments—he usually being the cause of them—makes any closer association inadvisable.

But Robert quite naturally takes to Alexander—with his apocryphal tales of the Zulu War, his eye for the ladies, his orotund views of human frailty, and his love for drink. He possesses those "faint ennobling virtues: never to be mean, to be kind, to inspire affection" (337). He delights in his own nature and in the act he has created. For of course we *hear* Alexander as well as see him. Like James Brodie and Lady Mary Fielding, he is a great rhetorical performer. He luxuriates in words and holds forth at great length, in his own highly distinctive idiom. When he defends Robert's right to practice Catholicism, he moralizes for half an hour "in the most heated and dramatic style: burning and immortal words flowed from his tongue, like 'freedom,' 'liberal,' 'tolerance,' 'free-thinker,' 'imperishable heritage' and 'the dignity of man' " (96). To defend Robert's right to try for the Marshall scholarship, he lectures the examiner:

My dear sir, it may be true that you have received these instructions. But I am here to countermand them. Not only in my own name, but in the name of decency, freedom, and justice. There are, after all, sir, even in this unenlightened age, certain essential liberties permitted to the humblest individual. Liberty of religion, liberty of speech, liberty to develop the gifts with which the Great Artificer has endowed him. Now, sir, if there is anyone low enough, and mean enough, to deny these liberties, I, for one, will not stand by and countenance it. (212)

On the day that Robert is confirmed, Alexander attends as a sort of cheering section—not for the love of God, but to annoy the Protestant relatives. Afterwards, he has lunch with Robert and an Italian family. He fascinates them with his memories of Italy—a country he has never actually visited—and drinks so much wine that several bottles have to be opened. The party breaks up when he puts his arm around the best-looking daughter of the Italian house. Through all of this Robert sees him as we see him: erratic, not always dependable, yet as one reviewer wrote, "still with an unquenchable zest for experience, an insatiable hunger for vital and beautiful things, an instinctive understanding of the human heart, especially a heart in trouble or in extreme youth."[3] Although an often vexing companion to the family, this Alexander Gow is one of the strongest influences in the early life of Robert Shannon.

We follow Robert as he moves from one sphere of influence to another until he matures enough in the process to bring about his own synthesis of experience at the end of the novel. Throughout these experiences his knowledge increases as he moves. His perceptions begin gradually to become more alert and articulate. Although the plot elements might be taken straight from the stock of any experienced writer of popular fiction, Cronin's understanding of people and events renders the situations new and fresh and satisfying. This judgment was echoed by many reviewers.

Social Progress, for example, gave unequivocal praise to *The Green Years* by saying that all that has gone into making Cronin an exceptional novelist is to be found in this novel: it uncovers "a segment of life as highly dramatic as any that Dr. Cronin has hitherto pictured."[4] The reviewer for *Harper's Magazine* said that Cronin makes "life in a family circle far more absorbing and exciting than many so-called adventure stories."[5] Like other perceptive critics of Cronin's work, William DuBois in the *New York Times Book Review* called the novel "a stirring and even eloquent story of a boyhood."[6] And in "artistry and quality," wrote the reviewer for the *Boston Herald,* this seems Cronin's best novel yet; Cronin captures the poignancy of his boyhood with "sure, sensitive skill."[7]

Although *The Green Years* was popular on both sides of the Atlantic, it did not entirely escape criticism. While the strength of the novel lies in its "Scotch honesty and aspirations," wrote the *Atlantic* reviewer, "the weakness . . . is its lack of force and subtlety, especially in times of crisis. It is curious that this novelist with medical training should dispose of death so quickly."[8] To others the plot was all too familiar and too carefully planned.[9] Like other chronicles, it has its redundancies and verbosity. In spite of these shortcomings, however, most critics agreed that the humanitarianism of *The Green Years* counterbalances its cynicism.

We should also note that some universality of experience makes the story interesting to readers of all ages, for we respond instinctively to experiences that could have been our own. As William York Tindall wrote,

the subject is convenient since every writer, like the rest of us, was first a child and then an adolescent, developing and struggling toward maturity. The subject is also agreeable since it is agreeable, as the poet said, to look back at troubles escaped or overcome. Mature at last, the writer, looking into his heart and at his past with all its trials and horrors, finds it easy to celebrate heart, past, and present maturity.[10]

The problems and joys and miseries are fundamental; everyone has been through them. We close the book with the feeling that Cronin intends to write another about Robert Shannon and his family.

Shannon's Way

As a bildungsroman, *The Green Years* asserted one set of expectations: that is, that the main character will grow and mature;

that crisis and conflict will be the means toward that growth to maturity; that questions of identity and self-understanding will be at the forefront of the novel; that they will take precedence over social adjustment and accommodation. In other words, Cronin expressed sympathy for young Robert Shannon in his struggle toward self-sufficiency and against a repressive environment. All of this background is necessary for our understanding of Robert's character as a mature research scientist in *Shannon's Way*.

The novel relates the "way" of Robert Shannon, now a young Scottish medic whose passion, even obsession, is research. He is still obscure (in spite of prizes won), still painfully poor, yet not nearly as shy, diffident, or retiring as when we last saw him. Thanks to the financial aid of old Alexander Gow, the hero, now twenty-four, has graduated from medical school with honors and the Lister Gold Medals. When the novel opens, Robert, Neil Spence, and Adrian Lomax are research fellows at the University of Glasgow under Professor Hugo Usher, the leading pathologist.

Complications begin for Robert when the professor forbids him to research the cause of a virulent influenza that is now sweeping through the neighboring village. In his absence, however, Robert isolates the bacillus causing the epidemic, checks its relation to undulant fever, and works to develop a preventive vaccine. But just as he is on the verge of an important discovery, he is reprimanded by Usher for disobedience. He quits his position, and his experiments are destroyed.

Robert seeks financial backing so that he can continue his studies, but persons and circumstances seem in collusion against him. From the university he goes to a small country hospital at Delnair, where staff politics stop his work; to the city slums, as assistant to Dr. James Mathers, a money-mad physician; and then to Eastershaws, a mental hospital where he finally completes his research.

All along Robert has been seeing Jean Law, the girl with whom he eventually falls in love. First she is his student, then his laboratory assistant. The obstacles to their love are as great as those to his work: a difference in religion brings opposition from her parents, strict Calvinists; she has a fiancé, Malcolm Hadden; and she intends to become a medical missionary. Yet she is responsible for Robert's regeneration. Just as he authenticates the discovery concerning the influenza, he learns that similar findings have been announced in print by an American woman. Worn out in spirit, mind, and body, he breaks down completely. He resolves to abandon his research and resign himself to the trivial routine of a general practitioner.

But then Jean, having recovered from a bout with scarlet fever, arrives with news of a lucrative position at the University of Lausanne and the promise of marriage to Robert. She returns to him, encourages him, and together they leave for Switzerland with no thought of failure, only the hope of eternal happiness.

The chronological position of *Shannon's Way* in Cronin's works is rather unusual. In discussing the genre of which this novel is an excellent example, William York Tindall notes that "from 1903 onwards almost every first novel by a serious novelist was a novel of adolescence."[11] *Shannon's Way*, however, was Cronin's eighth novel, written when he was fifty-two years old. Like *The Green Years*, it is the type of book we would expect the author to have written years earlier.

Cronin did, in fact, have *Shannon's Way* in mind early in his writing career. Some time in 1931, when he began work on what was to become *Hatter's Castle*, there came into his mind "a completely opposite idea, a haunting inspiration, both tender and moving, which would not let me alone," he told a reporter. It was to be a love story of "two obscure young people, students at a Scottish University, who loved each other yet were separated by the barrier of religion." Not until 1947 did he feel himself competent enough to do justice to such a "difficult" subject. He explained: "I say difficult advisedly, for I consider it the hardest test of all to write truly and convincingly of love. Most modern efforts in this direction seem to me to be artificial and unreal, dripping with sex, false sentiment and cheap emotion."[12]

Along with the love story, therefore, Cronin incorporates another theme: "In my opinion, what we need in our world today is an increase of tolerance, of the will to live and let live."[13] In *Shannon's Way* both of the principal characters are able to reconcile their personal difficulties and "come together in an ending which is really the beginning of their happy future."[14] Injustice and intolerance, man-made and enforced by profession and church—these are the fundamental themes that find expression in this novel.

Once again Cronin uses the autobiographical style to convey

"a greater sense of reality."[15] The narrative portrays doctors
as human beings; obviously Cronin has assembled out of his
own experience a cast of medical characters who are sometimes
amusing, sometimes pathetic, sometimes revolting. Although
he disavows a heavy autobiographical interpretation of the story,
he does admit to parallels between the characters and his own
experiences. Naturally Cronin was at home in writing about
the career of a young doctor. We have seen that the actual
subject of a doctor's life is one that affords material for many
human and dramatic scenes. One real experience formed the
basis for Chapter 2, Part 2, in which Robert performs an emergency operation on a child run over by a lorry. Also, Neil
Spence, one of the research assistants in the laboratory at the
university, was inspired by an acquaintance Cronin made while
in Paris: "a little ex-poilu, with a terribly scarred face, and the
sad, strained eyes of a man who finds himself lost and forgotten
in a heedless world." And Professor Challis grew out of a chance
meeting on a London bus with "a queer, charming old man
with a bird-like twinkle in his eye." Cronin was so fascinated
with his "eccentric, old-world charm"[16] that he followed him.
He never saw him again, but the impression left was vivid
enough to become a character in the novel.

There are also obvious parallels between this novel and Cronin's earlier work. Once again the hero is a doctor. Once again
the plot turns on the question whether two persons of different
faiths may marry and expect happiness. And once again Cronin
is on the side of tolerance. Also as in so many of his novels,
Shannon's Way follows a successful formula: a noble young man
places honor, integrity, and the love of pure science above the
materialists of the world. He is willing to suffer any humiliation
rather than compromise. His struggles are against the usual difficulties in a story of this kind, including incompetency in high
places, poverty, professional jealousies, lack of laboratory equipment, and so forth. Because of these similarities, many reviewers
complained that Cronin follows his formula "rigorously
throughout."[17]

In a number of ways, however, Cronin does avoid his lamenta-
ble tendency to repeat himself in his later novels. The most
obvious difference from the earlier doctor novels is that *Shannon's Way* lacks even a hint of humor. He uses melodrama to

highlight the discouragements, depressions, stresses, and strains that are the inevitable part of a research worker's life: his visit to a stricken village of Dreem, where he used to go as a boy on trout-fishing trips and where he is now collecting specimens; his impromptu tracheotomy upon Sim (the son of his old friend from the country, Alex Duthie), who then dies from diphtheria when the nurse leaves him unattended; his helplessness before the sight of Jean's illness; his feud with the hospital matron, Miss Trudgeon. It is no wonder that after all this, in a final act of despair over the failure of both his career and his personal relationships, he suffers a nervous breakdown.

Some of the difficulties spring from Robert's own impulsive, irascible, and unbending character. According to traditional norms of storytelling, he should be the villain; at any rate, he is certainly unattractive. At one time or another he hurts or betrays Jean, Callis, and Pollus. Aside from his fidelity to science, he exhibits few loyalties. He lies to Jean. He misleads her into believing that he wants to be a doctor. From her he also hides his Catholicism and his poverty-stricken background. When she confronts him with his lies, he tells her to go to hell. He also belittles his own religion, and is often too quick to judge other people. He is stubborn and inclined to think the worst of others. "That was my special quality," he says; "getting on the wrong side of people, acting against convention and the grain of decency, standing against the universe, belonging to no place, and to no one, but myself."[18] Some of his problems are inevitable when medical integrity meets the unprincipled and narrow-minded in the profession. Once again Cronin comes up with a gloomy diagnosis of many of the ills that afflicted the medical professional in postwar England of 1919. Laymen, doctors, nurses, hospital management committees—all are charged with a lack of integrity, foresight, and selflessness.

Yet for all this, Robert is far from being a contemptible figure. With his background from *The Green Years* before us, we are inclined to sympathize with him. We understand that certain causes as a child—his unpopularity, poverty, personal struggles—produced the effects seen in this later novel. To survive at all meant physical fights and mental subterfuge. He resorted to both; hence, he is the kind of person he is.

Robert is a brilliant young idealist, potentially a great scientist.

He has zeal and inquisitiveness. He lives in poverty because of his devotion to medical research. His temper is at times one of his most likable traits. Although he seems at first to be self-centered and insensitive to others, we follow his progress with increasing interest and affection. We begin to understand the reasons behind his actions. Of course, readers of *The Green Years* already understand them.

All of his life Robert has been a victim—of war, of politics, of bigotry, of malice, of petty plots, of accidents, and of coincidence. He has no money, no worldly ambitions. Material possessions and fame mean little to him. His only desires are a well-equipped laboratory and the privacy in which to pursue his studies. He describes himself as "a Catholic, who had strayed occasionally into the less dark corridors of scepticism, but who still, at heart, clung to his first belief" (45). Several critics have commented on the tragic elements in Robert's character.[19] His intellectual uncertainty, his uncontrollable passions, his deep-seated desires, rooted in pride, could lead to his own destruction. He violates Jean and then, in a torment of self-pity, permits himself to be seduced by Nurse Stanway. When he does repent, he repents only to himself. Robert may be seen as one of Cronin's figures of despair who is able to find happiness and peace of mind but only after great struggles.

Also new to his novel is the conflict over a love affair with a medical student whose background interferes with the romance. Unlike Robert's brooding dark-Irish, self-destructive temper, Jean Law's personality is buoyant, logical, and Calvinist. About her, Robert says: "Of the few young women I had met, she was the most supremely natural. She had . . . a striking, youthful, freshness. . . . But, more than anything, she looked, and smelled, so extraordinarily clean" (41). Unlike so many female students at the university who are in search of a husband, Jean wants to become a doctor in West Africa. She has grown up with a fanatic sense of duty to Calvinism. Her girlhood reading has been limited to *Good Words* and *The Pilgrim's Progress.* She has never been in a theater. Like her prototype, Christine (*The Citadel*), she is straightforward, loyal, and good.

One final difference is that in *The Citadel* Andrew Manson is tempted away from his standards by material success. In *Shannon's Way,* on the other hand, Robert's keen interest in his career stands out above everything else. Because of this one overriding concern, the life structure is not nearly as complicated here as it is in *Hatter's Castle* or *Three Loves* or *The Keys of the Kingdom.* The characters are few and present no particular difficulty in analysis. The action occurs within a comparatively short time (three years), and the outcome is obvious from the beginning.

In conclusion, *Shannon's Way* depicts a hero against the world who survives by perseverance, ingenuity, and sheer energy. He has his moments of self-pity and even despair, but these moments intensify our awareness of his plight. We see four stages in Robert's growth toward maturity. In the beginning he is unable to distinguish between his heroic dreams and hopes and the actual condition of his environment. Then follows a period of confusion and doubt as reality begins to intrude upon his dreamworld. Next he goes through a period of desperate struggle to preserve, through deceit and rationalization, his heroic image of himself and the world. In the end he solves his problem when he learns to see the world in its true light. Through all of this, wrote the reviewer for the *New York Times,* the narrative has "a sincere moral tone and brings to the conflict of good and evil a concreteness, a credibility, a sense that the narrator himself believes in the momentousness of the conflict."[20]

Conclusion

If *The Green Years* and *Shannon's Way* lack the sweep and excitement of his best work, they do show Cronin as a highly competent novelist, a convincing storyteller, and a writer interested in matters other than the spectacular, the fraudulent, and the corrupt. At the same time that they avoid the excesses of melodrama, they manage to be two of the most idealistic and patient of Cronin's books. They urge men and women to love one another, understand and forgive one another. They urge them also to solve their own problems so that civilization can begin to solve its problems. And they proffer hope, although not assurance, that those problems are solvable.

Chapter Seven

Variations on the Old

No serious reader can treat himself to very many of Cronin's novels without coming away with a strong impression of the moral force of the man and without the notion that his central concern is the quality of life and civilization in this world. It is not difficult to account for his faithful following into the 1950s. What is true of his earlier novels is certainly true of his next four: he is "relevant" in the best sense of the word. He writes with compassion in a world in search of a conscience; he believes in justice in a world of declining absolutes; he insists on integrity in a world of compromise; and he confronts our oldest problem, good vs. evil, in a world whose definitions have been eroded beyond recognition. In *The Spanish Gardener* (1950), *Beyond this Place* (1953), *A Thing of Beauty* (1956), and *The Northern Light* (1958), with varying success, Cronin's overriding lesson is human courage, a heroic facing up to overwhelming odds.

The Spanish Gardener

Since 1931, children have played a small but quite important role in Cronin's works: Nessie Brodie in *Hatter's Castle,* Mr. Chia's son in *The Keys of the Kingdom,* and Robert Shannon in *The Green Years* are examples. In his next novel, *The Spanish Gardener,* Cronin combines the simple story of a father's distorted love for his son with a favorite theme—that the neglected and ill-used child is also an imprisoned child. As an analysis of the perceptive and questioning innocence of its hero, explored and destroyed, this novel invites comparison with Henry James's *What Maisie Knew* (1897), Elizabeth Bowen's *The Death of the Heart* (1938), and L. P. Hartley's *The Go-Between* (1953).

The novel opens with the arrival of forty-five-year-old Harrington Brande and his nine-year-old sickly son, Nicholas, at the small seacoast town of San Jorge, Spain. There he hopes that the pleasant village will restore the health of his son—

ironically placed upon him by his own solicitude, supervision, and anxieties. But arrival at the village also symbolizes the doom of Harrington's own ambitions as American consul. After fifteen years with the State Department, he finds himself given a post he considers beneath his skill. Unrewarded in his career, forever receiving dull and routine assignments, the consul has also had bad luck in private life. His wife, Marion, has left him and several publishers have turned down his biography on an obscure French philosopher, Nicholas Malbranche. Lonely, frustrated, convinced that the world is responsible for his ill luck, Harrington is desperately determined to keep the love of his son.

San Jorge turns out to be a pleasant, amiable place. The consul's quarters, set on an estate overlooking the port and facing the Mediterranean, offer opportunities for the restoration of Nicholas's health. Determined to make the best of a bad association, Harrington hires nineteen-year-old José Santero, a young gardener with a simple, peasant joy in living. The gardener is a strong boy, the best pelota player in San Jorge, and an expert fisherman. He befriends Nicholas and cures the boy's ailments by exposing him to sunlight and fresh air. He also incurs the jealousy of Harrington, who sets out first to humiliate and then to destroy the peasant he regards as a rival for his son's affections.

Harrington's hatred for José is fed by the nasty implications of Dr. Eugene Halevy, a phony psychiatrist who implies that the boy's relationship with the gardener is unwholesome. Garcia, the butler, also plays on this hatred when he steals some of his master's jewelry and accuses José of the crime. Ultimately, José is killed when he leaps from a moving train en route to his trial. Harrington tries to catch José as he jumps, but the gardener loses his balance and fails to land clear of the train. José's death frees Nicholas from the prison of his father's possessive love and opens the way for the child to be reunited with his mother, the woman who could not endure the same possessive love of a vain man.

The tragedy of this story is that Harrington's egoism is so strong that he never learns from his mistakes. At the end we are told, "The edifice of his pride, though shattered, was not wholly destroyed, and from the noble ruins had sprouted this exquisite flower of martyrdom."[1] That Harrington was lied to

by Garcia and deceived by the sadistic psychiatrist does not
mitigate the torment he endures when he learns that he has
committed an irreparable wrong. He had already estranged his
wife; now he loses the love of his son. As in the case of James
Brodie, everyone who is associated with Harrington Brande
suffers in some way.

Harrington personifies self-deception. Obviously an egoist
and a snob, he venerates the aristocracy and believes himself
to be a humble, brilliant man of taste and discretion whose
talents are not appreciated by his superiors. In his mind he is
"a complete cosmopolitan, refined and polished by European
culture, a citizen of the world, in fact" (12). Although he cannot
understand why his wife left him, in a flashback we learn the
truth. He coerced her to marry him at a most vulnerable time—
just after her father had died. Then he did his utmost to prove
his love: choosing her books and flowers, planning her entertain-
ment, advising her on what people to know, helping her to
select dresses, and even livening up their evenings together
by allowing her to read from the book he is writing. When
he insists on hearing her opinion of his work, she says, "If
you really insist, Harrington, I'm afraid it bored me frightfully"
(59). We soon realize that she left him because of his selfishness,
because of his inability to regard her as an independent human
being. After she leaves him, Harrington bows in prayer for
all transgressions, particularly his wife's.

Once she has left Harrington, he transfers his possessive love
to his son. "Ever-watchful and protective," particularly at night
(16), he tries to amuse Nicholas by reading from Ackerman's
Book of Ornithology before he falls asleep. One of the descriptions
he reads to his son early in the novel describes ironically his
own unhealthy relationship with his son: "The birds are immensely vain of their feathers, and the male especially displays
great solicitude for its young" (18). In his neurotic, vain behavior Harrington joins the company of such characters as James
Brodie and Lucy Moore.

Unlike Harrington, the hired gardener is unspoiled by civilization. He is close to nature. He is a symbol of nobility: he rescues
a fellow human being from forces that would ensnare them
both, and then he makes the ultimate human sacrifice. To Nicholas, the gardener is "so young, so friendly, and so nice" (26).

He "chuckles" with delight (27) when he thinks of José's smile. From their first meeting he senses between them "a current of sympathetic understanding" (28). Invited to plant seedlings, he finds that "It was a lovely sensation to pick up the cool, green stem, to knead the soft, hot soil around the hair-like roots, to see the little shoot standing bravely up, resolved to face the world" (30–31). Nicholas's instinctive reach for all the good that José has to offer lifts him from the bondage imposed by a possessive, unseeing parent. The series version of Cronin's novel published in *Collier's* was entitled *The Prisoner*—a title that more appropriately, if less colorfully, epitomizes its theme.

Threatening Nicholas and creating for us heightened suspense are various kinds of abnormality. Garcia, for example, is the nightmare of every child, and perhaps of every adult: the deformed stranger, apparently harmless, offering friendship and requesting help, and suddenly demonstrating unexpected reserves of cruel strength. Nicholas's first meeting with Garcia gives him "a sensation curiously disagreeable" (14). His first night in San Jorge is haunted by dreams of "the dark, impassive figure of the butler" (19). He knows instinctively that Garcia is "a person who flattered only to deceive" (29). The mentally deranged servant, along with the sinister psychiatrist and the pompous, self-righteous and domineering father all prey upon the child; and this exaggeration of the evil influences at work around Nicholas is so prominent throughout the narrative that the effect is often that of a horror story instead of an entertaining study of conflicting human relationships.

In retrospect, perhaps we can see why the novel received only a lukewarm response from the public. On the one hand, Cronin's narrative skills are in evidence. That all of the events move in a single direction helps to explain the effects of clarity and simplicity that the narrative produces on a first reading. The story rushes forward, with the few interruptions—such as Harrington's memories of his married life or Nicholas's brief glances back to his days at home with his mother—serving less as breathing spaces for the reader than agonizing, dramatic reminders of how far events have gone. But the speed with which Cronin tells the story also explains the reason behind a major criticism of the novel: he does not take time either to develop fully Harrington's perverted personality, or to draw a complete

picture of José's simple goodness, which defies it. That these
two characters are "insufficiently realized," wrote Thomas Sug-
rue in the *New York Herald-Tribune,* "detracts from the sympathetic, moving figure of Nicholas, on which Doctor Cronin has
expended considerable of his artistry."[2] Lon Tinkle, writing for
the *Saturday Review,* echoed this judgment: "All these characters
are developed so skimpily . . . as to be mere puppets manipu-
lated adroitly by Dr. Cronin's sure hand. . . . The freight of
intended meaning is too heavy for such thin, pallid creations."[3]
    Some critics also found it difficult to believe in the variety
of plot elements. To the reviewer for *Wings,* for example, it
seemed incredible that a boy who has been smothered from
infancy could have "the spirit or stamina to defy overtly a father,
who had always terrorized him and victimized him by cold,
calculating, spirit-breaking domination."[4] To the reviewer for
Time the novel was "a minor classic, contrived and held together
with unnaturally stilted dialogue."[5] And to the reviewer for
the *Saturday Review* the novel's potential believability is weak-
ened by stock devices such as "the hurried and unexpected
out-of-town trip, the placing of stolen articles in an innocent
pocket, the villain's moll whose lies indict the virtuous, the
Eden-like retreat in the mountains, the pure hearts existing in
the midst of squalor."[6] In conclusion to all of this we might
say that *The Spanish Gardener* is more disappointing than bad:
its parts simply cannot redeem the whole. Yet it ought not to
be dismissed. Sometimes an unsuccessful work can be more
illustrative of a writer's approach, particularly in its weaknesses,
than a skillfully constructed, well-written novel. Perhaps Lloyd
Wendt, writing in the *Chicago Sunday Tribune,* captured best
its limitations:

If the reader accepts this tale for what it is, a rather nice horror story
set in a lovely garden, plus some insights into abnormal psychology,
he'll be satisfied and handsomely so. If he's looking for more he may
be disappointed. Most of the characters seem to be caricatures, completely incredible at times. The scenes, bright as they are, fade when
you close the covers.[7]

Beyond this Place

    There are three stories within the covers of Cronin's next
novel, *Beyond this Place.* One of them is placed in that land to

which Agatha Christie and Dorothy Sayers, among others, made such frequent excursions; that is, the detective story of a false conviction and the consequential undeserved suffering, the devoted search for the truth and the ultimate justification of the accused, with proper punishment of the real culprit. In *Beyond this Place* the story is based on a miscarriage of justice that really happened some decades earlier. Another story is that of a young man's struggle against heavy odds to obtain the release of his father from prison. A third story is rooted in the whole body of the British judiciary with their ancillary prosecutors and police, to present a passionate attack on the abuse of justice by the politically ambitious. Along with all of this, there are in this novel other elements that Cronin's readers have come to expect: "a strong, triangular love interest, a contrast between life of the rich and the poor, white virtue against black villainy, suspense, action, excellent pace and readability, and the rich, subtle and unexpectedly perceptive relationship between father and son."[8]

The novel is set in Northern Ireland and the Midlands city of Wortley in 1936, and opens on a deceptively peaceful note. Mrs. Burgess, a gray-haired "widow," welcomes her son, Paul, from medical school. Twenty-one years old, a thoroughly nice and intelligent young man, Paul applies for a summer teaching job to help his mother pay the bills, but she tearfully refuses to produce the necessary birth certificate. This leads to his discovery that his father is not dead, as he had been told, but is living as a condemned murderer who has spent fifteen years of a life sentence for the murder of a prostitute. Infuriated by his mother's, Pastor Fleming's, and daughter Ella's acceptance of his father's guilt, Paul goes to the scene of the crime, determined to find out the truth.

At Stoneheath prison Paul is moved profoundly by the sight of the grim and forbidding walls. A doubt rises in his mind and questions seem to challenge him to find the answers. How could the charming, companionable father of his remembered boyhood be capable of committing this horrible act? Why, if his father was a convicted murderer, was he not hanged? Had an innocent man been victimized and abandoned to this living horror? Desperately in need of answers to these questions, Paul delves into the past, digging out the facts of the trial and tracking down the witnesses. He learns that the doctor who first examined

the murdered woman had not been allowed to testify, that his
father could not have been responsible for her pregnancy, and
that two witnesses—Louisa Burt and Edward Collins—lied to
get the offered reward. He also learns that Prusty, the only
reluctant witness, refused to identify his father as the man running from the scene of the crime.

In reconstructing the tragic events that culminated in his father's imprisonment, Paul threatens the security of many people
connected with both the crime and the trial: his mother, who
believed his father was guilty, changed their name from Mathry
to Burgess, and raised Paul to believe him dead; Louisa Burt,
a housemaid who had positively identified his father as the killer;
Chief Constable Dale, an impeccably honest policeman who
overlooked positive evidence because he was so sure of the
prisoner's guilt; and Sir Matthew Sprout, for whom Rees Mathry's trial and conviction had been a springboard to fame and
wealth. The nearer Paul comes to the truth, the more perilous
becomes his own life. Sick and ill, he is brutalized by the police
and thrown into jail. But through the aid of an able newspaperman he eventually secures a new trial and the release of his
father. And all along, the Swedish girl, Lena Anderson, herself
a victim of a past tragedy, reassures Paul and nurses him back
to health.

Part detective story, part story of a young man's struggle
against great odds, and part story of legal and political corruption, *Beyond this Place* moves at a brisk pace. Certainly one of
the reasons for this is that the novel wears many of the trappings
of the conventional thriller detective story—particularly the
"manhunt" theme and an abundance of melodrama and violence. We also recognize the traditional surprise ending, the
essential clue that unlocks the mystery, and the elaborate plots
and subplots. And like so many writers in this genre, Cronin
uses the convention to mirror the frightened state of the world,
and to give the reader some assurance of hope.

Considered as a detective story, the novel is ingenious and
enjoyable, and its murder, prompted by sexual hypocrisy, satisfies the criticism laid down by George Orwell in 1946: "crimes
as serious as murder should have strong emotions behind
them."[9] The traditional detective story, in the very solving of
the crime, presents a view of life that is agreeable and reassuring

to the reader. It introduces him to a secure universe in which man is in control. It is an understandable and simple world. Usually the characters have simple problems that are related to the crime. Once the crime is solved, trouble vanishes. Life's confusion and frustrations are reduced to simple issues of good and evil. And good triumphs. The outcome is certain: the criminal will be defeated, the innocent will be cleared, and everyone who is innocent will be set for a cheerful future.

All this applies to Cronin's novel, except that questions linger long after we have finished reading it. What happens to a man during fifteen hopeless years in prison for a crime he did not commit? Can there ever be adequate redress even if the victim is set free? How does such a miscarriage of justice occur? If there are answers to these questions, if there is a happy ending to this grim yet fascinating story, Cronin wisely leaves it all to our imagination. The tale has a strange twist when years of prison and solitude have turned a careless and charming husband and father into a harsh, vindictive, and inhuman figure.

Beyond this Place has not only mystery, suspense, and intricate problems to be solved but also characters of some psychological depth, involved in perplexing situations that are more than puzzle plots. As the reviewer for *Booklist* wrote, "What might have been a routine detective story becomes an absorbing novel with convincing characters and sensitivity to ethical values."[10]

All of the characters are reminiscent of earlier creations. Paul, for example, is the typical Cronin hero: an impoverished, struggling, sensitive, decent young man for whom both Cronin and the reader have sympathy. Through him, Cronin tells a number of stories, including Paul's examination of his past, the case of Rees Mathry, the existing social system, and finally Paul's relationship to the world as both Paul *Burgess* and Paul *Mathry*. We see that he has been properly brought up by a strait-laced, self-sacrificing mother. He has happy memories of his father as a companion in sailing paper boats when he was a small boy, and therefore he cannot believe that his father could have committed such a crime. We feel sympathy for him because he was brought up in ignorance of his father's fate and because, like any son, he is determined to learn the truth. In one vivid moment, for example, Paul pours over old newspaper files and comes upon "a page of photographs—reproductions of the victim—a pretty, simpering young woman with a padded fluffy chignon; of the contemptible informer, a weak-faced, weedy creature, with sleek hair plastered in a middle parting; of the weapon—a German razor."[11] We share with him such intimate moments of discovery as well as of pain—when, for example, he is forced out of his job, left ill and penniless.

Also reminiscent is Lena Anderson, a quiet, attractive girl in whom Paul is interested until he hears that she has had an illegitimate child. Although he is slow to appreciate her, Lena provides the needed support: she finds him in a bread line, takes him home, feeds him, gives him a room, and after learning his story, interests a newspaperman in arousing public opinion to the point that Parliament takes action, Paul's father is released, and the case is reopened for a complete investigation. Other characters who stand out sharply include the ambitious prosecutor, the hardheaded police officer, the girl who was a key witness against Paul's father, the discredited officer who would not accept the verdict and gave Paul some clues, and Paul's father, a bitter, brutalized caricature of the father of his boyhood days.

But the novel's deeper attraction lies in its social significance— a nonpolitical, Dickensian sort of protest against injustice. Cronin himself supplied a starting point for this approach when he said:

I felt I must write this book because the present system of trial by jury, which has remained unchanged for many centuries, does not present the best or the fairest method of judiciary processes . . . The system is liable to grave errors, particularly when, as so often happens, the case for the prosecution is presented by a strong and capable advocate and that for the defense by someone less competent and with less ability to play upon the emotions of the jury, who, incidentally, may be uninformed and, in some cases, unintelligent individuals.[12]

As we have seen, because a mistake was made, the entire established order, from the lowest policeman right up to the top government official, appears determined to keep the mistake hidden and let the innocent suffer. To accomplish this end they abuse the very powers given them to insure that justice shall be done. Cronin also gives us dark glimpses of life behind English prison walls, where life is so bleak that murder within the prison is frequent. Inmates emerge more like animals than men. We see crooked prosecutors, politically controlled judges, dishonest witnesses, and wealthy evaders of justice. Once again, Cronin finds his scoundrels among the pillars of the established branches of society.

We have seen that a number of features—the mystery story, the vivid characterization, the social commentary—contributed to this novel's popularity. And yet we must conclude that *Beyond this Place* is another of Cronin's less successful books. It is carelessly and sometimes awkwardly written, with several errors in time sequence and several loose ends. And there are many improbabilities. Would or could a British police chief threaten to close down a newspaper? Would British police spy on a young man who had committed no crime and try to frighten him into leaving town just to please an influential public prosecutor? Would a murderer, even allowing for his natural excitement, leave behind him at the scene of the crime so striking a clue as a purse made of human skin? Questions such as these diminish the credibility of the story.

Although some critics commended the novel—"expertly handled melodrama," "lavishly evoked emotion," "sure best seller" equal to Cronin's earlier successes—most reviewers found the melodrama, old-fashioned plot, and stiff, pedestrian prose too much for their taste.[13] Accordingly, Cronin was accused of "misusing his talent," of being in a "very unbuttoned mood"[14] when he wrote the novel. *Beyond this Place* was described in various reviews as "stiff and earnest," "old-fashioned," "strung on a thread of cliché," "stilted," and the like.[15] One reviewer noted that the language with which Cronin reports the dismal events is so Victorian he wonders why the novel was not set in 1876 instead of 1939:

"Alas" and "without avail" are followed by "certain acts that are unmentionable." The rain is "pitiless," the heath is "accursed," tears are "scalding," and cries are "wild" and "inarticulate." Disappointments are, of course, "cruel," sobs are "choking," and matters that are futile are "unutterably" so. Paul is swept by "storms of emotion" and "convulsive shudders" except for those moments when he is "crushed by the weight of disappointment" and "biting his lips fiercely."[16]

A Thing of Beauty

In his next novel, *A Thing of Beauty*, Cronin returns once again to the theme of the dedicated man, to write of a man who, like the great Paul Gauguin, sacrifices everything for art—family, friends, social position, career, ultimately his own life—and leaves to others a heritage of beauty. It is a theme about which Cronin cares deeply, and to which reviewers responded favorably. *Kirkus Review* called it "the best thing Cronin has done since *Shannon's Way*."[17] The *Library Journal* praised it as "a magnificent picture on a vast canvas."[18] John Barkham in his *New York Times* review headed "Persecuted for His Art" called the novel "an object lesson in the power a writer can infuse into a story when he becomes deeply involved in its theme."[19] And the *Saturday Review of Literature,* under the title "A Painter's Peregrinations," credited Cronin for giving his readers "a carefully constructed story, carefully described characters, and carefully evoked landscapes."[20]

The focus of all this praise is the story of Stephen Desmonde, son of Bertram Desmonde, Rector of Stillwater, Sussex. The time of the story is just before and just after World War I, during the troubled era of postimpressionism, when the battle for modern art is raging in the studio, the art gallery, and the press. It is a time when young artists are proud to live "daringly," to acknowledge as their masters—and to imitate—Monet, Degas, and Renoir. It is a time when, according to a long tradition of the social life of the English upper class, only three careers lay open to the sons: the Army, the Law, the Church. To fall below these, to be touched by "trade" or the vulgarities of studio or stage, is definitely to lose caste.

When Stephen comes down from Oxford, in 1912 or 1913, it is expected that he will take orders and succeed his father in a living that has been held by his family for generations. In an effort to please him, Stephen works at a mission in London's East End, where he meets Jenny Dill, a fresh, ignorant, sensible young cockney. He even studies religion, attends a seminary, and works for a while as a curate. But when his attempt to serve God in the slums ends in failure, he runs off to Paris at the urging of a fiery Welsh artist-friend, Richard Glyn. Neither the draw of the family homestead, the countryside round about, the security of a comfortable inheritance and living, nor the lure of marriage to Lady Broughton's daughter, Claire, can counterbalance Stephen's obsession to paint. In what follows we are shown the gradual conversion of an upper-class Englishman into a dedicated artist.

Generously enough, his father gives Stephen one year, with a regular allowance, to discover the folly of his ambition and return to Claire. When the year is over, however, Stephen comes home only to announce that he is committed, body and soul, to painting (as indeed was Cronin to his own writing). His father's heart comes close to breaking, and Claire finds herself pushed toward another loveless marriage. All of this might have been easier to bear had there been any proof that Stephen is talented. But according to the expert opinion of a member of the Royal Academy, his paintings are outrageous.

Nevertheless, for the next ten years Stephen serves his apprenticeship, working first as an English tutor to a grocer's children and then as a charcoal portrait artist with a French circus. He also wanders about Paris (where he studies) and Spain (where he makes a pilgrimage to art centers), all the while starving, enduring hardships, even contracting tuberculosis, but always painting. Along the way he falls in love with a trick cyclist, Emmy Berthelot, who taunts him and spurns him while having affairs with other men.

After refusing to participate in the war, Stephen returns to England where he causes a furor with his realistic antiwar paintings for a war memorial. Influenced by Goya's *Desastres de la Guerra,* Stephen turns out a bitter commentary upon the wastes of war well calculated to outrage his fellow citizens and to get him convicted under the obscenity act for exhibiting salacious pictures. The misunderstood painter tries to defend his art against the indignant (and ignorant) local burgesses, but the panels are burned—just as, years later, his work is rejected by the Royal Academy for straying too far from its own mediocrity.

Driven beyond despair and racked with illness, Stephen returns to the East End of London. There he meets again and eventually marries Jenny Dill. Her devotion and care see him through his remaining years and his creative talent as an artist is gradually recognized by the public. But here Cronin adds a twist that we do not find in some of the novels about Vincent

Van Gogh and Gauguin: Stephen's work is recognized as fine and important *before* he dies. In retaliation for their years of neglect, however, Stephen refuses to sell the art dealers a single painting.

All along, of course, the Rector of Stillwater is bewildered, angered, disappointed, and at last forgiving of the son whose strange disobedience and defiance of convention have brought such sorrow into his own life. Yet even at the end he can feel only sadness in the universal acclaim of his son's genius: "thinking of the pain and disappointment of a lifetime crowned too late, he wondered if it had all been worth it. . . . What was beauty, after all, that men should martyr themselves in its pursuit, die for it, like the saints of old?"²¹ However, Stephen did live an intense and full life—as this story of his failures and triumphs, his stubborn courage, his conflict with vested interests of official art, his loves and marriage, makes abundantly clear. If he knew sorrow and frustration, he also knew the inner peace and joy of a dedicated life.

In bare outline the plot is admittedly trite and worn. The story of Stephen Desmonde could be that of several hundred sensitive young heroes of novels, for long before 1956, when *A Thing of Beauty* was published, both the artist and the adolescent had become conventional subjects of fiction. From the beginning of this genre in the late eighteenth century to the present, the artist-hero is an easily recognizable character type. He is, Maurice Beebe writes, "always sensitive, usually introverted and self-centered, often passive, and sometimes so capable of obstructing himself mentally from the world around him that he appears absent-minded or 'possessed.' "²²

In Stephen we do find these and other familiar features of the artist-hero tradition: dissatisfaction with the domestic environment, estrangement from a Philistine father, a conviction that art is a vocation superior to time and place, the discovery that he cannot go home again, and withdrawal to an ivory tower of sorts. *A Thing of Beauty* also shares a number of parallels with another artist-hero novel, Somerset Maugham's *Of Human Bondage* (1915). Like Philip Carey, Cronin's hero is a shy, reluctant divinity student who throws over the ministry to become a poverty-stricken artist in Paris. He, too, becomes enthralled by a cheap, illiterate girl and degrades himself by spying upon her, much as Philip does with Mildred Rogers. In both of their careers there is a Paris period, a Spanish period, and later an English period.

A significant difference between the two novels is that unlike *Of Human Bondage,* in *A Thing of Beauty* art is stronger than sex and the more demanding life partner. Cronin has reversed the myth common to the late nineteenth century in which woman is viewed as the femme fatale, the destructive element capable of destroying a man's career. Although both Philip and Stephen find themselves entrapped by women who are unworthy of them, in Philip's case the discovery of his human bondage destroys whatever artistic aspirations or abilities he may have; in Stephen's case he passes successfully through the experience and finds himself the better for it. Unlike Philip, Cronin's hero begins to rise in aspirations, opportunities, and creativity as he leaves behind Claire, the bourgeois girl, and spends time with Jenny, the uneducated cockney.

Aside from these innovations, what makes this novel memorable? Perhaps Cronin himself supplied the answer when he wrote of it: "While it is difficult for an author to appraise his own work, I can say in all honesty that this book, more than any other, was written from the heart."[23] Possibly he was referring to the very fine character of the Rector, who with his deep longing for a close relationship with his son, reminds us of the Consul in *The Spanish Gardener.* Here Cronin was writing from a strong trait in his own character. He may have been referring also to his own struggles as a literary artist. The problem of artistic creativity, how it may thrive or be thwarted in a range of circumstances, recurs at every crucial moment in the novel. Like Joyce Cary in *The Horse's Mouth* (1944), for example, Cronin wonders about a painter's private pursuit of a beauty often not recognized until after he has died. What is the nature of the artistic genius? What kind of people are they, those who sacrifice every material reward and ignore or even outrage every conventional ideal of behavior in order to paint pictures according to their own private conception of beauty? In this particular case, Cronin focuses upon Stephen's efforts to do his work decently and honestly in an atmosphere of cant, commercialism, and competition. It is a subject with an abiding interest for Cronin—as an artist himself—and for us, even if some of the details are dated; but as we read the book it becomes clear that we are being invited to regard the struggles of men like Stephen as instances of a problem that assaults sensitive human beings throughout the modern world. Add to this theme Cronin's own pacifist leanings—which come through forcefully in Stephen's character—and we can begin to understand some of the reasons for Cronin's comment about the book.

Also, the book conveys fully the impression of "solidity" because Cronin knew the artistic world of his day. He knew it not merely in the factual sense, which enabled him to define the exact shade of malice in the Royal Academy's report, or the peculiar talent that Stephen shows in his three periods. Along with this factual accuracy is the sense we gain from the novel that the experience it presents has been earned, absorbed, stamped with the authority of pain. For as a collector of paintings himself, Cronin knew a great deal about the problems and humiliations of painters whose experimental or avant-garde pictures represent revolutionary changes in technology and taste, and he drew upon his knowledge to develop *A Thing of Beauty*. The poor, hungry, rebellious artist with his strange pictures may be a genius, he seems to be saying; he should be respected. Although the present generation may not like his work, quite likely the next one will. Remember Frans Hals and Rembrandt, Van Gogh and Gauguin, Modigliani and Stephen Desmonde. "We are the only ones who matter" (217), says Stephen as Cronin's mouthpiece. The creation of truly enduring beauty, the genuinely great artists, matter to posterity as no soldier or citizen of repute can.

Stephen paints because he is creative, not because he wants fame, worldly success, or money. He is the artist ever at odds with society. Whether or not he is successful by society's standards does not matter to him. This theme—the conflict of the artist and society in a modern world—poses the paradox of injustices and freedom. Society has not fulfilled its obligation to the creative genius. Its academies and national galleries support the dead academician, not the living creator. This is one element of injustice in the world, the price the artist pays for his freedom to create. As the epigraph to the novel makes clear, "Not only is fame (and until recent years even liberty) denied to men of genius during their lives, but even the means of subsistence. After death they receive monuments and that by way of compensation."

The Northern Light

Early in 1958, when he was nearly finished with the writing of his next novel, *The Northern Light,* Cronin remarked to an interviewer from a Canadian newspaper, "There is nothing new to write about, only a new way to write about the old things. That is the gimmick."[24] His impulse to write a "gimmick" novel may have arisen from a not uncommon criticism at that time— that Cronin was failing to bring fresh territory within his imaginative range. In any event, *The Northern Light* demonstrates his thesis. It is a gimmick book with a skillfully twisted plot and an appealing theme: righteousness, after a formidable challenge, may at least hope to emerge with a share of victories over evil. *The Northern Light* was an instant success, but this time without the benefit of much controversy.

When Jane Voiles read it, she found "a dignity and a generous tone throughout."[25] Fanny Butcher, writing for the *Chicago Sunday Tribune,* said: "Whether or not you are interested in newspapers and battles for circulation when you start the novel, you will be before you get too far into it."[26] And in his review for *Catholic World,* Riley Hughes called it "that rare thing in a novel today, a satisfying and exciting story."[27] All of these reviewers also honored Cronin's powerful story about the tribulations of a good man facing up to the wickedness, stupidity, or bigotry of the world. But unlike his earlier novels and his accustomed themes of medicine and religion, this work concerns a provincial British newspaperman's fight against overwhelming odds to keep his paper and to defend his integrity.

The novel's title—not to be confused with the Belfast paper published by the Ulster Anti-Prohibition Council—is the name of a newspaper that, since 1785, has been published by the Page family in the English city of Hedleston, Northumberland. Its present owner and editor is Henry Page, a small, middle-aged man keenly devoted to his community, his newspaper, decent journalistic standards, and freedom of the press. He is a much-respected figure, a symbol of stability and rectitude who shuns sensationalism and instead prides himself on a sober presentation of the news. In a sense, Henry *is* the town: quiet, a bit old-fashioned, committed to the faith that the England that once was must some day be again, and doing his part in the editorials to bring that about. As he writes:

In its own limited sphere, [this newspaper] follows the great papers that have maintained their principle—papers that lead and educate the people, and try to create intelligent citizens, rather than a nation of gaping primitives reared in a mixture of sex, sensation and scandalous gossip.[28]

But Henry is disturbed when Leonard Nye, head of a powerful newspaper syndicate, offers to buy the paper for £50,000. Why should the owner of the *Gazette*, a sex and scandal sheet with a circulation in the millions, be interested in a homey, provincial newspaper? The answer is known soon. Vernon Somerville, a London publisher, has decided to move into town because he has learned that a nuclear reactor plant and a housing development are coming into the Hedleston area—providing a huge new field for circulation and profits. Unfortunately, Henry's newspaper had missed the story because its reporter somehow was unable to determine what the initials "N.R.W." stood for in a dispatch from Parliament. The rest of the plot concerns the efforts of the Somerville forces to push Henry out of business, and his valiant efforts to keep his paper alive without resorting to Somerville's tactics.

Henry's refusal to sell out precipitates a desperate struggle to defend not only his property but also his beliefs and the lives of the people he loves—including Cora, the "common" girl with a loving heart, who is trying to forget the shameful secret of her past; her brilliant husband, David, who is haunted by his own fears; and Henry's wife, Alice, who is afraid that they will lose their home and position.

As Henry struggles against the terrible pressures brought upon him, he sacrifices everything but his integrity. He mortgages his house, sells his collection of rare Staffordshire china, borrows a few hundred pounds from his assistant editor, and even asks some of the veteran employees to take a salary cut. Meanwhile, his wife and daughter, both socially ambitious and indifferent to his ideals, turn against him. Many of his staff desert to his rival. The townspeople become avid readers of the lurid, deplorable stories published in the rival paper, *The Light*. And his suppliers, his financial sources, his security, all collapse. Two of the press lord's hatchet men are then sent up from London. When they find they cannot buy out Henry, they are prepared to drive him out. The most damaging way to attack him, they discover, is through his family. They come after his wife and daughter after they fail to destroy him by trying to cut off his paper supply, by hiring his assistants, by abusing the legal system to deprive him of his printing plant, and by throwing him into confrontation with uncharitable, hardheaded bankers. But Henry saves himself with an ingenious idea: when his printing plant is seized, he puts out a daily mimeographed sheet. The townspeople are so impressed with his valor that they switch back to his side. And although his victory ends in personal tragedy—his wife and daughter commit suicide—he has maintained the principles of human decency and goodness for which he has fought all his life.

Once again, here are the causes we have come to expect in Cronin's novels—personal integrity, nonconformity, tolerance. The problem of human integrity, how it may thrive or be thwarted in a range of circumstances, recurs in all of his fiction. Here Henry's struggle against seemingly unconquerable fate and his impregnable faith in the right are investigated with the usual Cronin thoroughness. In his portrayal of the ruthless encroachments of a yellow-journalism monopoly, the writing is vivid, the inhumanity disgusting, the brutality terrifying. The tone is that of an exposé, yet another assault on modern life. The importance of this novel is that it brings new subject matter into Cronin's canon. The ministry, the medical profession, the creative artist, the struggles of youth—all have been depicted by a compelling and often crusading pen. But now he turns his attention to the newspaper world and the efforts of a serious journalist to do his work decently and earn his living honestly in an atmosphere of cant, commercialism, even corruption.

This new subject matter exists within the familiar Cronin pattern: the person who stands for a conservative way of life pitted against representatives of everything restrictive, hypocritical, wasteful, and narrow in society. The man who appears in the opening pages of the novel is already a man caught in the grip of a fate that it will be the novelist's task to make real to him and to us. He is Henry Page, an honest, reliable, hardworking man whose unbelievable patience with suffering turns him into the embodiment of Job. He is average in his share of human limitations but remarkable in his dedication to integrity—in spite of all impediments and beguilements.

Chapter Eight

The Later Phase: Minor Fiction

By now it is clear that the 1940s marked the apogee of Cronin's literary career. While there was little slackening of his output— he continued to write and publish until the end of his life— and while some of his later novels (*The Judas Tree*, for example) contain fine work, came close to the sales, and aroused some of the stir of his earlier books, nothing he wrote in his last years really matched the remarkable achievement of *Hatter's Castle, The Stars Look Down, The Citadel,* or *The Keys of the Kingdom.* Thus "minor fiction" is perhaps a polite way of saying "Cronin's less successful fiction." The term may be taken to cover at least four novels[1] of varying length: *The Judas Tree* (1961), *A Song of Sixpence* (1964), *A Pocketful of Rye* (1969), and *Desmonde* (1975).

The Judas Tree

Like *Hatter's Castle, Three Loves,* and *The Spanish Gardener, The Judas Tree* is the story of an individual beset by a supreme egoism. In this case, retribution comes to a man who in every crisis allows himself to be forced into decisions that result in his material success and moral impoverishment. He manages to bring grief not only to himself but to two women, mother and daughter, who count most in his life.

Rich, charming, and accomplished, but lacking in good judgment and a sense of consideration for others, widower David Moray is at fifty-five a man especially attractive to women. He prides himself on being a self-made man. Once a struggling young medical student in Glasgow, he had eagerly taken full advantage of a chance encounter with the daughter of a drug manufacturer. Although later she died insane, he rose quickly from the depths of poverty to financial success and retirement in Switzerland, detached from the dangers and anxieties of the working world. Suavely elegant, impressively wealthy, a con-

noisseur of food and the arts, he has surrounded himself with
a costly collection of paintings and objets d'art. When not off
to London, Paris, or Vienna, he passes the time with aristocratic
but impoverished Frida von Altishofer, who owns a run-down
castle across the lake. She is no longer young, but she has the
style David has come to admire. He has even given thought
to the idea of marrying her.

One evening at a party, without the slightest premonition
of impending disaster, a chance remark about Scotland reminds
David of a situation that for years has caused him a deep sensation of guilt. We learn that in order to marry the heiress he
had ruthlessly abandoned a girl he loved and had promised to
marry. Now, thirty years later, he is determined to rid himself
of that guilt by going back to Scotland and asking for her forgiveness.

When he returns to Scotland, however, he finds that Mary
Douglas, his old love, has died and that he is helplessly in love
with her image, daughter Kathy. She is a dedicated young nurse
living near Edinburgh who plans to leave shortly for service
at a remote medical mission in Africa. David attempts to ease
his conscience by lavishing on her the affection he had withheld
from her mother. After an idyllic interlude in Vienna and Switzerland, he even offers to accompany her to Angola, where
they will marry and he will work as a doctor in the danger
zone near the Congo border. All is arranged, but, during Kathy's
brief return to Scotland, David sees this plan of giving up his
comfortable life as nothing more than middle-aged madness
on his part. In panic, he marries the fortune hunter, Frida. The
novel ends tragically when Kathy drowns herself and David
hangs himself, predictably, on the Judas tree growing outside
his bedroom window.

Reviewers commended various features of this novel. The
Boston Sunday Herald called it "a tour de force in which the
author gives credence, understanding and impact to the ethical
problem of an individual who will not face up to himself or
the obligation he incurs."[2] Robert C. Healey, writing for the
New York Herald-Tribune, found in this novel "much less emphasis on melodrama and external action, much more on introspec-
tion and psychological development," but in David's character
he found "little more than a puppet." Healey also points out

that in order to dramatize David's culture, Cronin lists French, German, and Italian comments and talks of "food, décor, travel and the arts."[3] That such a cultivated man would carry guilt over a jilted first love for thirty years is hardly convincing. Parton C. Keese, in the Worcester *Telegram,* also called David "one of the most weak-minded heroes" in fiction, though interesting to read about.[4] To Aileen Pippett in the *New York Times Book Review,* on the other hand, the novel is "strong stuff, skillfully administered by a practiced hand."[5] She commented on Cronin's "adroit" mixture of romance and realism, his "convincing" reports on life among the ignorant poor and the cultured rich, his "appropriate" notes of "moral fervor and elegant sophistication," but she too finds many improbabilities in the novel, particularly in David's character.

What seems of special interest here is the organic cohesiveness of Cronin's technique. In this novel he develops pervasively but elusively a correspondence between natural object and human event and attitude. The object is the Judas tree. As with several of Cronin's books, the central symbol is signaled by the title, and its meaning is vitally connected with the implications of the novel itself. On the second page we are told of David's splendid orchard with its seventeen varieties of fruit and, more important, his "greatest botanical treasure."[6] Before long Cronin makes his meaning explicit:

the great, gorgeous Judas tree that rose high, high above the backdrop of mountain, lake, and cloud. It was indeed a handsome specimen, with a noble spreading head, covered in spring with heavy purplish flowers that appeared before the foliage. All his visitors admired it, and when he gave a garden party it pleased him to display his knowledge to the ladies, omitting to reveal that he had looked it all up in the Encyclopedia Britannica. "Yes," he would say, "it's the *Cercis siliquastrum* . . . the family of *Leguminosae* . . . the leaves have an agreeable taste, and in the East are often mixed with salad. You know, of course, the ridiculous popular tradition. In fact Arturo, my good Italian, who is amusingly superstitious, swears it's unlucky and calls it—*l'albero dei dannati*—" here he would smile, translating gracefully— "the tree of lost souls." (8–9)

That the tree is central to the story is clear, even if its significance is not, ironically, until the end. Later, Cronin will confirm and expand the meaning of his symbol. As we learn more about David, we discover that he is indeed a lost soul, and that his status as such relates directly to his betrayal of Mary Douglas thirty years before. The tree comes to symbolize David's own individual hell in which he is imprisoned. Cronin himself metaphorically resolves the central problem of the book in a revealing passage near the end. David is standing alone, close to the tree, grieving over the death of Kathy, and Cronin tells us:

He ceased to meditate and, under the moving branches of the tree, raised his head in a sudden, upward glance. The swing, with its long ropes, was oscillating gently in the breeze. Seductive . . . the motion— it fascinated him. Following the gentle movements across the face of the moon, he simply couldn't take his eyes away. The faint rhythmic creak of the metal cleats began to beat a little tune inside his brain. Reality had left off; illusion was brightening his eyes. He was beginning to understand everything in a peculiar and interesting way. This extraordinary calm was the most marvelous sensation he had ever experienced. And now he was talking to himself, in a quiet, confidential manner, carefully forming the words: restitution, complete vindication, the court of last appeal—absolving all guilt, restoring his ideal self. He stood there for a long time smiling to himself, enjoying his triumphant acquittal in advance, before he decided it was time for him to produce the evidence. (223)

The controlling symbol of the novel, signaled by the title, expresses perfectly both the author's intent and his method of carrying it out. Without question, the most persistent emphasis in *The Judas Tree* is on David's coming to terms with his guilt, and his character is conclusively revealed through his relationship with four women. Mary Douglas is a Scottish girl whose early love scenes with David are some of the most touching Cronin has written. Her daughter Kathy is a dedicated nurse, but her youth and the fact that she is almost a living replica of her mother at the same age combine with David's obsession of "redemption" to draw him to her. An extraordinarily complex girl, Doris Holbrook's erratic and erotic behavior is a symbol of something more than the spoiled daughter of a self-made man that she first appears. Finally, Frida von Altishofer is a cultured and strong-minded woman with just that ruthless disposition capable of breaking down David's irresolute nature. Set against the background of Scotland, Switzerland, Vienna, and Connecticut, the novel revolves around these characters with mounting tension. The most remarkable transformation is that of David Moray. We are fascinated by his youthfulness, his affluence. We admire his talents as a young doctor and respect him for his rise from poverty. We also sympathize with him, particularly when we consider his humble beginnings. But David is not an admirable fellow. We disapprove of his abandonment of Mary Douglas, of his exploitation of Doris Holbrook, of his obsession with Kathy. With love comes responsibility, and he shirks his responsibility. There is a kind of poetic justice near the end, when Frida succeeds in pulling him away from Kathy. What is more, his suicide seems to be the logical conclusion, for he takes that final step to escape the consequences of his own blind self-adulation.

A Song of Sixpence

Written from the first-person point of view, *A Song of Sixpence* is the deeply felt story of Laurence Carroll, an unbelievably unspoiled child who is, in many respects, Cronin himself. The story begins in 1900, when the boy is six years old, and carries him through his adolescence. In a strongly Protestant Scotland, Laurie's Catholic mother and father suffer from the rigid bigotry of their neighbors and the consequent isolation from friends and relatives. At first the boy is content at home: he is, like Robert Shannon of *The Green Years,* a quiet child, sensitive but bright, sheltered and loved.

But then occurs the death of his father from tuberculosis, and the poverty that ensues, the tentative assistance of his relatives and the gallantry of his mother who still shelters him as much as possible from the adversities that follow. First, his only friend is run over by a train. Then he is sent to live with Uncle Simon, a Catholic priest whose housekeeper, Miss O'Riordan, is a devout Catholic. Then his mother experiences problems at work, and Miss Greville, the eccentric benefactress, who initiates him in botany, cricket, and cutlers, goes out of her mind. While working in Uncle Leo's textile warehouse, Laurie is induced by bookie friends to run in a rigged foot race. He loses.

Then his shopgirl cousin, Nora, tries to seduce him, but fails. By means of a mismanaged abortion she lands him in jail. He emerges to compete for the Ellison Essay—for which he had been tutored by his old village schoolmaster—and he wins it. By the end of the novel Laurie admits that he is like everyone else, "the victim of every sentient mood, the unwilling slave of my own emotions."[7]

Critical reaction to the novel was at best lukewarm; most reviewers lamented Cronin's habit of repeating himself. G. E. Grauel wrote: "A. J. Cronin says that this new novel is more representative of his real literary aspirations than anything else he has written. Though writers are not always the best judges of their own work, the book does superbly achieve an unaffected warmth and human genuineness that are extraordinarily satisfying."[8] The reviewer for the *New Statesman,* on the other hand, found in the novel little continuity. Except for the hero, he wrote, the characters are "pawky, twinkling, galvanized for the occasion." He was particularly annoyed by the big "gap" between "the teller now and the credulous, rather soft child."[9] To the *Critic,* the novel was "pleasant if superficial [and] escapist fare."[10] And to the reviewer for the London *Times Literary Supplement,* Cronin's story was "rather impeded" by circumstances much like David Copperfield's. He wrote:

> the gallant widowed mother and threat of a vulgar remarriage, the romantic attachment which founders squalidly, the series of eccentric friends and guardians. The monster with the ugly head is class not sex. The worst betrayals are social. Poverty is genteel, and not till near the end, when the autobiographical detail stiffens the sentiment, do the real miseries and frustrations reveal themselves. It is a pleasant, competent book, and only slightly dull.[11]

Obviously, *A Song of Sixpence* is a deeply personal work. While it is not the true-life story of the Cronin who had struggled as a child, it is the story of the sort of "little" person, lonely and searching for fulfillment, with whom Cronin could not avoid comparing himself. Furthermore, the novel does reflect several autobiographical parallels. Both the hero and Cronin suffered from religious bigotry in a predominantly Protestant town. Both were lonely and longed for companionship. Both lost their fathers at an early age and were subsequently compelled to live with relatives. Both suffered from oppressive poverty. Both were unhappy with the routine of their jobs and sought to break out of them. Perhaps most fundamental, both experienced the abiding restlessness (a dissatisfaction with the status quo) and optimism that mark the ambitious person. In that respect the novel also invites comparison with *The Green Years,* for it utilizes some of the same situations and conflicts. These parallels, and the autobiographical similarities, perhaps help to account for its popular success among readers well acquainted with Cronin's life and works.

A Pocketful of Rye

In *A Pocketful of Rye* Cronin returns to the familiar territory of Scotland and Switzerland and to the familiar subject of doctors and their patients. Dr. Laurence Carroll, hero of *A Song of Sixpence,* emerges again—still feckless, still irreverent, but now a physician and practicing at the poverty level in a small Scottish town. By a combination of sheer good luck and some highly unethical schemes, he escapes the hated socialized medicine of the United Kingdom and secures a comparatively soft position at the Maybelle, a small children's clinic outside Zurich. His dominant attitude is, "On velvet at last after eight years of mucking around in the worst kinds of general practice."[12]

Laurie takes full advantage of his new position, living for the moment and squandering his medical talent. We see him display the minimum of interest in children, shirk his responsibilities, love his rye whiskey, use women, and ignore the Church. Hilda Muller, matron in charge, eyes him with suspicion. But he ignores her, and they operate the Maybelle at a respectful and amicable distance from each other.

All that changes after Cathy Davigan, a former lover, brings her seven-year-old son, Daniel, to the clinic for treatment. In a flashback we learn of Laurie's early experiences at Scottish Levenford and his contacts with the forbidding Canon Dingwall and the young, naive Francis Ennis. The latter shares his father's hopes that he will succeed him in medicine, and give up the love of Cathy Considine to become a priest. Cathy marries Laurie's old rival, Daniel Davigan, who is killed in an accident.

When Danny becomes ill, Ennis sends him and his mother to see Laurie at the clinic.

Then begins the strange saga of old love renewed in the face of bitterness, Danny's treatment for myeleocytic leukemia, chess games in the snow-covered mountains to satisfy the addiction of the curious Danny, Laurie's dalliance with an airline hostess, the disclosure that Davigan's death was not an accident, and that Danny is really Laurie's son. At the end, Laurie experiences a spiritual conversion after reading in a gift book Francis Thompson's "The Hound of Heaven" (a poem Cronin had always loved). As a result, he returns to a humble post in Switzerland to take up Dr. Ennis's practice. There he will also try to renew his youth with Cathy and nourish his thwarted ambition and his sense of humor. As an "essay" on the Catholic conscience and the Church's rulings on marriage, *A Pocketful of Rye* is thematically consistent with Cronin's earlier novels.

Although the novel was received enthusiastically by his publishers and bought by the Literary Guild in America, the Book-of-the-Month Club in Britain, and the Crown Book Club in the Netherlands, it was not a critical success. In reporting its publication in paperback two years later, *Publishers Weekly* wrote: "The suds may sell it although they didn't in hardcover."[13] True, a few watchers announced the new novel joyously. But in the late 1960s it was not the praise ("a sensitive, poignant story," "demonstrates once again Mr. Cronin's remarkable ability to convey and to celebrate the drama, the pathos and the glory of human existence," "superb" characterization)[14] that predominated. It was the snide phrases ("just pleasant reading," "predictable rather melodramatic plot," "pious novel . . . dreary as ever," "preposterous")[15] that stung the memory and affected sales. *Choice* could find a few passages to approve, but was overall antagonistic. It advanced what was before long to be the prevailing judgment: "Any library can do nicely without this novel; avid Cronin fans will not want to read what has happened to their author and his hero."[16]

Desmonde

The *Library Journal* called Cronin's next novel, *Desmonde,* "an enjoyable narrative of a half-rogue, half-saint which should please traditionalists."[17] The novel marks a departure for Cronin in that he inserts himself as "A. J.", one of the main characters. *Desmonde* opens with A. J.'s private Jesuit school reminiscences of Desmonde Fitzgerald, a quick-witted, handsome, charming youth who wants to become a Catholic priest. After he wins the coveted Silver Chalice for his Spanish seminary at a singing competition in Rome, he is sent to a village in southern Ireland. Desmonde's letters recount how he masters a cleric's vocation within and outside the seminary. He also becomes involved with the leading church patron, Geraldine Donavan, who inherited a giant whiskey concern after an operatic career, and with her daughter, who seduces Desmonde from his vow of chastity and traps him in an unfortunate marriage, only to divorce him later. Only when he learns to make full use of his marvelous voice does he begin to build a new life. He redeems himself by volunteering for missionary work in India.

Conclusion

A discussion of Cronin's last four novels—*The Judas Tree, A Song of Sixpence, A Pocketful of Rye,* and *Desmonde*—ought not to divert our attention from the important and permanent work that came out of his earlier period. Missing from these books is some of the excitement the creator conveys when he is making discoveries, when he is finding fresh materials and new insights rather than reproducing old ones. The heroes are variations on earlier characters whose life pattern is the same: there is a problem, it is met, conquered, and dissolved, with different degrees of consequences. However, while it would be unwise to assess Cronin on the strengths of this writing, and unprofitable to linger over it for long, it does present us, in brief, with certain rudiments of his imagination. As one reviewer wrote for the *New York Herald-Tribune:* "It is all too easy to deride the mountains of clichés, the stilted dialogue, the cardboard characters and the simple, uncomplicated emotions that have characterized the [later] novels. The fact remains that he is an immensely successful popular storyteller, whose novels are somehow immensely readable."[18]

Chapter Nine
Epilogue

Virtually everyone is willing to say that A. J. Cronin gave promise of becoming a great writer. He possessed a brilliant mind, a breathtaking skill with narration, and a strong imagination. His novels were read because he made his characters live and his scenes happen, however improbable the one or the other. What is more, he had a willingness and a disposition to spend long hours at the perfection of his craft, a deep interest in the traditions of prose fiction, and always a powerful ambition to create compelling and significant books. As a phenomenon in literary history, Cronin deserves to be taken seriously.

And, indeed, during his lifetime he was granted at least a measure of the reputation for which he seemed destined. Hugh Walpole, John Galsworthy, Charles Auchincloss, and Clifton Fadiman were among his friends and admirers. Among the reading public, Cronin's reputation seemed even more secure, his books selling over twenty million copies worldwide. If not the subject of a great deal of serious critical attention, Cronin did receive from notable reviewers many marks of distinction. He was portrayed as a courageous man who led an active and adventurous life; as an individual who struggled for subsistence and finally won sensational success; as a friend of the poor and a crusader for social justice.

In the final years of his life, when he lived in Switzerland, his novels continued to sell in the hundreds of thousands. On hearing of his death, T. Saito, one of the faraway admirers, commented in a letter to Cronin's son Vincent that "Mr. Cronin has taught us, Literature is Joyness and Literature is at the same time Sadness, but we, Human Being [*sic*], should select Joyness from Sadness through Literature."[1] And a school teacher near Corinth wrote: "I am so sorry because a useful and great man passed away. . . . Cronin taught us humanism and love through his pages."[2] Fifty years of writing fiction have left Cronin with a faithful following.

If we can still read Cronin with profit, why then has he been ignored by so many who determine literary reputations? There are perhaps three main reasons for this history of neglect—a neglect at or near the top, we should notice, rather than among the wider novel-reading public, who have always seen to it that his works remained very much in print. The first reason stems from the apparent flaws in Cronin's own sensibility, talent, and attitude, and we must frankly admit to these flaws. He was a keen and perceptive writer but not a developing writer in the fullest sense of the word. *Hatter's Castle, The Stars Look Down, The Citadel, The Keys of the Kingdom,* and perhaps *The Green Years* make a group of novels that present Cronin at the pitch of his powers. In each he shows that peculiar discernment of the novelist which can fix the authentic individuality of a character and simultaneously establish it solidly in a social world. Each work represents an increased perception of the novel as a weapon of social criticism and an art form. Since 1950, however, his development follows a winding course, occasionally recalling his earlier successes (*The Judas Tree*), once or twice successfully shaping something new (*A Thing of Beauty*). Although the later novels—those published after 1958—deserve to be studied and praised, too many are ephemeral. He undertook to repeat the same situations, characters, and themes in a style somehow grown dated and stale.

Secondly, and more recently, literary fashion seems to have moved away from Cronin. For the "New Critics" his novels hold no interesting ambiguities, intentional or unintentional; there are no puzzles, no obscure allusions, no "levels of meaning" within them. What can be said about a writer whose characters are predictable, whose themes are announced forthrightly and regularly, whose symbolism is plain and transparent? Only the reviewers continued to give him notice.

A third factor that has told against Cronin's repute is more difficult to assess. Some critics are unable to find either literary or intellectual grace in a man whose books were read by millions, who wrote for *Reader's Digest,* who always headed the best-seller lists, and who was the darling of book clubs. Perhaps this inattention is in some cases snobbery. These critics rarely ask themselves what invisible virtue sustains such a wide readership or what moral vision kept Cronin going in spite of critical disfavor.

If he has never been short of detractors, Cronin has had his defenders, too. First, Cronin's appeal to the reading public lies in his fulfillment of the most fundamental requirements of the successful writer: that he be an accomplished storyteller. Second, it is a people's literature with a mass appeal because it embraces such profound themes and conflicts as good vs. evil, life vs. death, and altruism vs. selfishness. Third, his appeal rests on his humorous and sympathetic understanding of human nature. His literature confirms rather than condemns humanity. He writes as a friend who reassures and accepts his reader. Fourth, he creates a variety of original, fascinating characters and types who are believable and memorable. Last, though unsophisticated about certain aspects of literature, he works within a tradition, consolidating and building on the work of others.

Cronin is perhaps most obviously traditional in the Victorian form of his novels, which were written on a larger scale than most written today, with an abundance of characters, incidents, details, and events. With such a scale he was able to give a comprehensive picture of his society, and the problems he dramatized were real and important. Himself the victim of social injustice, he denounced it with courage. He never forgot the indignities and hurts he had sustained as a youngster, and if his pride at having beaten the system left him with a weakness for dramatizing his achievement, he was an outspoken critic of social callousness and brutality. Thus his novels belong decidedly to the class of purpose or problem novels. "His message was compassion for the downtrodden, encouragement for those striving to be true to their aspirations. The distinctive note was hope."[3] Many readers found in his novels a relief from the melancholic, oppressive, and depressive philosophy that seemed to have swept away so many contemporary writers.

There is nothing Pollyannaish about this philosophy, no bleating optimism. While he does not use sex and violence or sadism as staples of his depictions, his works contain a tension and an indication that life is a rather seamy mess. Like many novelists before him, he does on occasion take evident pleasure in some of his rascals, whose overflow of vitality leads them to hazard strange and slippery paths. But he can never be said to have written a human comedy. His view is much too serious for that. We do not have to read far in any of his novels to realize that Cronin will protect virtue and punish wickedness, keeping his favorites jeopardized but seldom irreparably harmed. We learn to anticipate a pattern of apparent catastrophes and hair-breadth escapes, to recognize exaggerated fears or parodies of danger, and, above all, to trust our omnipotent and ubiquitous narrator. The suspense, ultimately, is not *if* but *how* he will bring his favorite characters through the storm to the happy shore.

The structure of most of his novels—one or more subplots with an emphasis on the episodic narrative—also follows tradition. Discursiveness was an asset especially to serial writers like William Makepeace Thackeray, Anthony Trollope, Charles Dickens, and Rudyard Kipling. Although Cronin himself seldom wrote for serialization, most of the works he had read as a boy emerged in that form from the magazines of the day. He absorbed their manner as he absorbed food and drink, with the following result: his proclivity for ending chapters at their most climactic point. The well-worn plot line of exposition, defining event, rising action, crisis, falling action, resolving incident, and denouement is just as much a part of his first novel, *Hatter's Castle,* as it is of his last, *Desmonde.* To Cronin as realist, the novel was a dramatic device.

A strong believer in environment, too, he portrays "place" both geographically and psychologically, with varying mixtures between. His villages invite comparison with Oliver Goldsmith's and Trollope's; his London owes something to George Gissing's realism and even more to Dickens's humanity; his "bizarre, murky macabres" with psychotic overtones, remind us again of Dickens or, even more, of the Brontës. His interest in minute and specific depiction is both logical and pertinent, and his power to create exceptionally vivid and finely detailed pictures actually improved as his artistry matured.

To give dramatic effect to his narratives, Cronin introduced odious and loathsome characters, and made vice more hateful by contrasting it with innocence and virtue. We find in his novels, therefore, three or four widely different character types: the innocent child, like Robert Shannon; the horrible or grotesque foil, like James Brodie; the grandiloquent or broadly humorous fun maker, like Alexander Gow; and the tenderly or powerfully dramatic figure, like Francis Chisholm. Characters on the side of right are humble, kindly, generous, benevolent;

those on the side of wrong are hypocritical, miserly, avaricious, intolerant. And like the writers of the old moralities, Cronin makes his figures symbolic. Within the conventions he uses, his novels have a universal application. Not that Cronin was of Dickens's caliber, for example, but his art has deep roots. It represents something well beloved and indubitably valuable—the English novel in the grand tradition. For all of these reasons it seems appropriate to conclude that Cronin will continue to be read and valued.

Also pointing to lasting and significant aspects of his work is his successful television series, "Dr. Finlay's Casebook." As depicted in two collections of short stories—*Adventures of a Black Bag* (1969) and *Doctor Finlay of Tannochbrae* (1978)—the series recapitulates the central themes of his early novels, including the underlying frustrations of life, culture as a force of corruption, and love thwarted or satisfied. Through a wealth of situations Cronin examines artistically the problems and challenges of the general practitioner's relation to society, obliging us to reevaluate our own attitudes to ourselves and to others. A fairly common assumption among writers and literary critics is that what fiction ought to do is tell the truth about things, or as Edgar Allan Poe says, express our intuitions about reality. Viewed in this way, these stories are a kind of instrument for coming to understanding.

Like so many of Cronin's heroes, the good doctor has no illusions about himself and very few about other people. He is honest, idealistic, forthright, ready to speak his mind, unwilling to compromise his principles. Of Finlay, Dr. Cameron (his superior), and Janet (their housekeeper), Vincent Cronin says: "[this triad of characters is] a most interesting, I would even say important, creation, and the permutations worked on it are among the best things my father did."[4] Cronin's depiction of the general practitioner—never far from suffering, life, and death—certainly reminds us of the best of his early fiction. And his well-observed characters, rich authentic dialogue, and original storytelling are the pivotal points here as well as in the middle years of his career. A combination of all these qualities is rare in twentieth-century English fiction. In many of the formal tributes that appeared just after his death, there was an acknowledgement that he would be remembered for both his "big novels" and his television series.

Again and again as we review Cronin's writings, we are reminded of him at earlier stages in his career. His life was all of a piece, and varied as were his interests, they can all be traced back to his childhood and youth: in the boy at Cardross and the young man at Glasgow University we see his character formed. The seeds of his future concerns were sown then. The gifted lad, however much handicapped by the circumstances of his birth, received a good education and rose high in the professional class. But Cronin could have done well in any subject and to any task to which he applied himself. It was only by accident, or, as he would have said, providence, that he achieved fame as a writer: he simply obeyed the creative urge. But it was also because of his unique abilities that the novels were produced. With his self-assurance, outstanding stamina, hope for the world, strong sense of duty and service, and wide general knowledge, Cronin was the right man at the right time. And he never lost his enthusiasm for telling stories. "He knew the life-histories of everyone in the village [of Montreux] from the postman to the grocer. This material, reworked in his imagination, provided stories for his grandchildren, and for books, up until his eightieth birthday."[5] Of all the comments that have been made about his life and writings, the following by his son perhaps best sums up the achievement it represents within its genre, while at the same time placing it in its literary and historical context: "His early novels had been classified as indictments of social injustice in the Dickensian tradition. That was partly true. . . . But there was much more to his novels than exposure of wrong, or even than lovable characters and superb story-telling. They were informed by a deep religious faith."[6]

In his latter years, when he could no longer leave his home, Cronin watched "Le Jour du Seigneur"—televised Mass from a French country village "which reminded him of his boyhood."[7] He was befriended by Canon John Roger Fox of the abbey of St. Maurice, and according to Vincent Cronin the succession of final events went like this: "Soon after being admitted to the Valmont Clinic, where Rilke had spent his last days, he received the sacrament of the annointing of the sick from Canon Fox, after which the mental anguish induced by sclerosis yielded to a serenity remarked on by all. He who had done much to bring Christ's message to the nations died peacefully on the feast of the Epiphany."[8]

Notes and References

Chapter One

1. *Adventures in Two Worlds* (New York, 1952), p. 265. All subsequent page references in this chapter are to this edition.
2. "Profit By My Experience: Reward of Mercy," *Reader's Digest* 39 (September 1941): 35.
3. "February Publication Planned for A. J. Cronin's First Non-Fiction," *Davenport Times,* 12 January 1952, p. 3.
4. "Cronin, A(rchibald) J(oseph)," *Current Biography 1942,* ed. Maxine Block (New York: H. W. Wilson Co., 1942), p. 167.
5. Ibid.
6. Ibid.
7. Ibid.
8. Edwin Francis Edgett, "A Novel by a Doctor about a Doctor," *Boston Evening Transcript,* 11 September 1937, p. 1.
9. In a letter from Vincent Cronin (21 June 1982) he writes, "Dr. Cameron and Tannochbrae are fictitious names, though they probably correspond to counterparts in my father's life."
10. Ibid.
11. "Cronin, A(rchibald) J(oseph)," p. 168.
12. Ibid.
13. Ibid.

Chapter Two

1. Herman Melville, *Moby Dick* (New York: Norton, 1967), p. 108.
2. Hugh Walpole, "Books Abroad: London Letter, June," *New York Herald-Tribune Books,* 28 June 1931, p. 9.
3. L. A. G. Strong, "Fiction: the Rough and the Smooth," *Spectator* 146 (30 May 1931):870.
4. Anon., "New Novels," *Times Literary Supplement* (London), 11 June 1931, p. 464.
5. James Agate, "New Fiction," *Daily Express* (London), 10 June 1931, p. 67.
6. Percy Hutchinson, *"Hatter's Castle:* A Novel in the Great Tradition," *New York Times Book Review* (19 July 1931), p. 4.
7. John T. Frederick, "A. J. Cronin," *College English* 3 (November 1941):123.

8. "Books: Books in Brief," *Forum* 86 (September 1931): x,
xii; "Fiction," *Booklist* 28 (September 1931):26; Francis Lamont Rob-
bins, "The New Books," *Outlook and Independent* 158 (22 July
1931):378.
9. *Hatter's Castle* (New York, 1931), pp. 5–6. All subsequent
page references in this chapter are to this edition.
10. Letter to Hugh Walpole, 6 July 1931; quoted in Hugh Walpole, "Books Abroad: London Letter, June."
11. "Cronin, A(rchibald) J(oseph)," *Current Biography 1942*, p.
168.
12. Fred T. Marsh, "The Pride of Possessiveness," *New York
Herald-Tribune Books*, 3 April 1932, p. 5.
13. Gerald Bullett, "New Novels," *New Statesman and Nation*
3 (5 March 1932):300.
14. Review of *Three Loves, Springfield* (Mass.) *Republican*, 29 May
1932, p. 7.
15. "Notes on Fiction," *Nation* 134 (1 June 1932):632.
16. "New Novels: *Three Loves,*" *Times Literary Supplement* (London), 25 February 1932, p. 130.
17. L. A. G. Strong, "Fiction," *Spectator* 148 (27 February
1932):298.
18. *Three Loves* (Boston, 1932), p. 139. All subsequent page references in this chapter are to this edition.
19. "Lucy Moore's Three Loves," *New York Herald-Tribune Books*,
5 April 1932, p. 5.
20. "Notes on Fiction," p. 632.
21. Basil Davenport, " 'Unhand Me, Villain,' " *Saturday Review
of Literature* 9 (20 May 1933):605.
22. George Dangerfield, "Decline and Fall," *Saturday Review of
Literature* 7 (18 July 1931):972; Ola M. Wyeth, "*Grand Canary*: A
Novel by A. J. Cronin," *Savannah News* (16 July 1933), p. 18.
23. *Grand Canary* (Boston, 1933), pp. 7–8. All subsequent page
references in this chapter are to this edition.
24. For the inspiration behind the ship's name, see "Cronin,
A(rchibald) J(oseph)" in *Current Biography.*
25. Percy Hutchinson, "Dr. Cronin's Gift for Narrative," *New
York Times Book Review,* 14 May 1933, p. 6.

Chapter Three

1. "Fiction," *Irish Times,* 11 October 1935, p. 11.
2. "The Book of the Week," *New York News,* 22 September
1935, p. 3.

3. Hugh Massingham, "New Novels," *Observer* (London), 11 September 1935, p. 5.

4. Percy Hutchinson, "The Clash of Capital and Labor." *New York Times Book Review,* 22 September 1935, p. 1.

5. Joseph Henry Jackson, "New Novel by Author of *Hatter's Castle* Is Work of High Quality," *San Francisco Chronicle,* 29 September 1935, p. 4.

6. *The Stars Look Down* (Boston, 1935), p. 19. All subsequent page references in this chapter are to this edition.

7. Robert Louis Stevenson, "Will o'the Mill," in his *The Merry Men* (London: Chatto & Windus, 1887), p. 32.

Chapter Four

1. *The Citadel* (London, 1937), p. 186. All subsequent page references in this chapter are to this edition.

2. "Books: Doctor: England's New Dickens Reports on Former Profession," *Newsweek* 10 (13 September 1937):34–35.

3. Review of *The Citadel, Lawrence* (Mass.) *Tribune,* 27 August 1937, p. 5.

4. "New Books," *Leader* (London), 2 September 1937, p. 7.

5. "Cronin's New Novel," *New Chronicle* (London), 15 September 1937, p. 7.

6. "The Book Mark," *Glasgow Forward,* 21 September 1937, p. 8.

7. Review of *The Citadel, Lawrence Tribune,* p. 5.

8. "Dr. A. J. Cronin on Doctors," *Times* (London), 10 November 1937, p. 11.

9. Ibid.

10. Ibid.

11. Frank Swinnerton, "Fiction," *Observer* (London), 3 November 1937, p. 6.

12. Mary Ross, review of *The Citadel, New York Herald-Tribune Books,* 12 September 1937, p. 1.

13. Mabel S. Ulrich, M.D., "Doctor's Dilemma," *Saturday Review of Literature* (London) 16 (11 September 1937):5.

14. William Carlos Williams, "Books and the Arts: A Good Doctor's Story," *Nation* 145 (11 September 1937):268.

15. Ralph Thompson, "Books of the Times," *New York Times,* 10 September 1937, p. 21.

16. "Doctor's Dilemma," *Times Literary Supplement* (London), 14 August 1937, p. 591.

17. See "Book Chatter," *Jacksonville* (Fla.) *Times-Union,* 26 Sep-

tember 1937, p. 3; "Books: Doctor: England's New Dickens Reports on Former Profession," p. 34.

Chapter Five

1. Christopher Morley, *"The Keys of the Kingdom,"* Book-of-the-Month Club News (July 1941), p. 3.
2. John Cotton, *Keys of the Kingdom of Heaven* (London: Heinemann, 1911), p. 12.
3. *"The Keys of the Kingdom:* In His Third Best Seller Scotland's Writing Doctor Takes Faith for His Theme," *Life* 11 (24 October 1941):64.
4. Ibid.
5. Ibid.
6. Ibid.
7. Ibid., pp. 64, 65.
8. *The Keys of the Kingdom* (New York, 1941), p. 15. All subsequent page references in this chapter are to this edition.
9. Review of *The Keys of the Kingdom. Atlanta Constitution,* 10 August 1941, p. 13.
10. Mary Ross, "A Most Appealing and Memorable Book: Cronin's New Novel Will Be the Subject of Wide Discussion," *New York Herald-Tribune Books,* 20 July 1941, p. 1.
11. Wilbur Larremore Caswell, review of *The Keys of the Kingdom, Churchman* 155 (1 September 1941):21.
12. Frank Fitt, "The Saint As a Best Seller," *Christian Century* 58 (3 September 1941):1081.
13. "Jubilant Praise Greets *The Keys of the Kingdom!"* *Gastonia* (N. C.) *Gazette,* 2 August 1941, p. 3.
14. "Cronin, A(rchibald) J(oseph)," *Current Biography 1942,* p. 169.
15. Ibid.
16. John C. Cort, "Communications," *Commonweal* 34 (29 August 1941):447.
17. "Cronin, A(rchibald) J(oseph)," p. 169.
18. Weidman, Jerome, "Books: Dr. Cronin's New Novel Full of 'Incredible Hokum,' " *PM's Weekly,* 20 July 1941, p. 44.
19. Wilbur Larremore Caswell, *Churchman,* p. 21.

Chapter Six

1. *The Green Years* (Boston, 1944), p. 73. All subsequent page references in this chapter are to this edition.

2. Florence Haxton Bullock, "Cronin's Enchanting Novel of a Boy's Life," *New York Herald-Tribune Books,* 12 November 1944, p. 3; J. F. Cronin, "Growth of Character," *Cincinnati Enquirer,* 18 November 1944, p. 6; Charles Dancoke, S. J., "Cronin's *Green Years* Merits Few Laurels," *Milwaukee Herald Citizen,* 2 December 1944, p. 4; Harry Hansen, "The First Reader," *New York World Telegram,* 13 November 1944, p. 23.

3. John Erskine, "Fine and Warmly Human Story of an Old Man and a Lad," *Chicago Sun Book Week,* 12 November 1944, p. 25.

4. Thomas Franklyn Hudson, review of *The Green Years, Social Progress* (December 1944), p. 16.

5. Katherine Gauss Jackson, "Books in Brief: Fiction," *Harper's Magazine* 196 (September 1944):126.

6. William DuBois, "Scenes from a Frustrated Boyhood," *New York Times Book Review,* 12 November 1944, p. 3.

7. Alice Dixon Bond, "The Case for Books," *Boston Herald,* 15 November 1944, p. 14.

8. "Boy Against the World," *Atlantic Monthly* 174 (December 1944):127.

9. Review of *The Green Years, Boston Globe,* 29 November 1944, p. 30; review of *The Green Years, Chicago News,* 13 December 1944, p. 8; Harry Hansen, "The First Reader," p. 23.

10. William York Tindall, *A Reader's Guide to James Joyce* (New York: Farrar, Straus & Giroux, 1959), p. 51.

11. William York Tindall, *Forces in Modern British Literature: 1885–1956* (New York: Vintage Books, 1956), p. 146.

12. "A. J. Cronin Talks About *Shannon's Way,*" *Wings* (August 1948), p. 5.

13. Ibid., pp. 5–6.

14. Ibid., p. 6.

15. Ibid., p. 7.

16. Ibid., pp. 7–8.

17. C. W. Terry, "Scotch Sour," *New York Times,* 18 July 1948, p. 12.

18. *Shannon's Way* (Boston, 1948), p. 287. All subsequent page references in this chapter are to this edition.

19. "New Cronin Book Relates Doctor's Bitter Struggles," *Oakland Tribune,* 25 July 1948, p. 6; Francis X. Connolly, "Literary Guild—August Selection," *Best Sellers* 8 (1 August 1948):97; Marguerite Page Corcoran, "New Books," *Catholic World* 167 (August 1948):474; James Gray, "Author Cronin's Bound to Make Hero Suf-

fer," *Chicago News,* 28 July 1948, p. 6; Mary Exley Presson, "Oft-Wounded Knight: A. J. Cronin Creates More Masterly Misery," *Cleveland News,* 21 July 1948, p. 4.
    20. C. W. Terry, "Scotch Sour," p. 12.

Chapter Seven

    1. *The Spanish Gardener* (London, 1950), p. 250. All subsequent page references in this chapter are to this edition.
    2. Thomas Sugrue, "Smother Love of a Father," *New York Herald-Tribune Books,* 27 August 1950, p. 6.
    3. Lon Tinkle, "Serpent in Eden," *Saturday Review of Literature* 33 (9 September 1950):20.
    4. Review of *The Spanish Gardener, Wings* (November 1950), p. 5.
    5. "Books," *Time* 56 (4 September 1950):84.
    6. Lon Tinkle, "Serpent in Eden," p. 21.
    7. Lloyd Wendt, "Cronin's New Novel Is Grim and Incredible," *Chicago Sunday Tribune,* 27 August 1950, p. 3.
    8. Sterling North, "Sterling North Reviews the Books," *New York World Telegram,* 20 July 1953, p. 7.
    9. George Orwell, "Decline of the English Murder," in *The Collected Essays, Journalism and Letters of George Orwell: In Front of Your Nose: 1945–1950: IV,* ed. Sonia Orwell and Ian Angus (New York: Harcourt, Brace & World, 1968), p. 101.
    10. "Fiction," *Booklist* 50 (1 September 1953):13.
    11. *Beyond this Place* (Boston, 1953), p. 111. All subsequent page references in this chapter are to this edition.
    12. Review of *Beyond this Place, Trenton Times,* 28 June 1953, p. 13.
    13. Richard Sullivan, review of *Beyond this Place, Chicago Sunday Tribune,* 19 July 1953, p. 3; Louise R. Miller, "New Books Appraised: Fiction," *Library Journal* 78 (15 June 1953):1148.
    14. John Barkham, "Even the Judge Was a Conniver," *New York Times,* 19 July 1953, p. 5.
    15. "Books: Briefly Noted: Fiction," *New Yorker* 29 (1 August 1953):59; John Barkham, "Even the Judge," p. 5; Jean Holzhauer, "The Price of Reticence," *Commonweal* 58 (17 July 1953):374.
    16. Charles Lee, "Fraying Margins of Error," *Saturday Review of Literature* 36 (25 July 1953):14.
    17. "Fiction," *Kirkus* 24 (15 March 1956):217.
    18. Robert W. Henderson, "Fiction," *Library Journal* 81 (15 April 1956):911.

19. John Barkham, "Persecuted for His Art," *New York Times Book Review,* 20 May 1956, p. 4.

20. Ben Ray Redman, "A Painter's Peregrinations," *Saturday Review of Literature* 89 (2 June 1956):12.

21. *A Thing of Beauty* (Boston, 1956), p. 312. All subsequent page references in this chapter are to this edition.

22. Maurice Beebe, *Ivory Towers and Sacred Founts: The Artist as Hero in Fiction from Goethe to Joyce* (New York: New York University Press, 1964), p. 5.

23. P. McL., "From Dr. Cronin's Heart," *Free Press* (Winnipeg), 26 May 1956, p. 7.

24. Robert Fulford, "Dr. Cronin at Work," *Telegram* (Toronto), 7 June 1958, p. 3.

25. Jane Voiles, review of *The Northern Light, San Francisco Chronicle,* 1 June 1958, p. 24.

26. Fanny Butcher, review of *The Northern Light, Chicago Sunday Tribune,* 1 June 1958, p. 1.

27. Riley Hughes, "Books: Novels Reviewed by Riley Hughes," *Catholic World* 187 (June 1958):229.

28. *The Northern Light* (Boston, 1958), p. 5. All subsequent page references in this chapter are to this edition.

Chapter Eight

1. In a letter from Vincent Cronin (30 June 1984), he writes: "*Lady with Carnations* [1976] and *Gracie Lindsay* [1978] were never intended for publication as books. They are lightweight magazine stories. Only because his publishers pressed him did my father, then an old man, reluctantly consent to have them issued in book form. I think in any serious assessment of Cronin's oeuvre, these stories should just be mentioned in passing."

2. Alice Dixon Bond, "A. J. Cronin's *Judas Tree* Conveys His Spiritual Values," *Boston Sunday Herald,* 25 November 1961, p. 17.

3. Robert C. Healey, "A Suave Egoist and His Guilty Past," *New York Herald-Tribune Books,* 8 October 1961, p. 84.

4. Parton C. Keese, "Storyteller of Finesse," *Worcester* (Mass.) *Telegram,* 8 October 1961, p. 11.

5. Aileen Pippett, "Memory of Love," *New York Times Book Review,* 15 October 1961, p. 46.

6. *The Judas Tree* (Boston, 1961), p. 8. All subsequent page references in this chapter are to this edition.

7. *A Song of Sixpence* (Boston, 1964), p. 224. All subsequent page references in this chapter are to this edition.

8. G. E. Grauel, "Fiction," *Best Sellers* 24 (1 October 1964):258.

9. Christopher Salveson, "Et in Somalia Ego." *New Statesman* 68 (31 July 1954):155.

10. Robert Burns, "Another Key, Another Kingdom," *Critic* 23 (October 1964):74.

11. "Other New Novels," *Times Literary Supplement* (London), 27 August 1964, p. 769.

12. *A Pocketful of Rye* (Boston, 1969), p. 22. All subsequent page references in this chapter are to this edition.

13. Elizabeth Erdos, "Paperbacks: Fiction," *Publishers Weekly* 199 (11 January 1971):64.

14. Pat Diorio, review of *A Pocketful of Rye, El Paso Times,* 12 October 1969, p. 6; Starling Ennis, "Cronin's New Novel Again Shows His Skill," *Birmingham News,* 28 October 1969, p. 6; G. H. Pouder, "Books: Some Suggestions of the Macabre," *Baltimore Sunday Sun,* 5 October 1969, p. 5D.

15. "Brief Reviews," *Critic* 28 (November 1969):169; "Language & Literature: English and American," *Choice* 6 (February 1970):1752; Teddi Gibson, "Cronin Still Having a Medicine Ball," *Cleveland Press,* 8 May 1970, p. 12; Jane Dennis Washer, "Just Pleasant Reading from the Pen of Cronin," *Richmond Times-Dispatch,* 28 October 1969, p. 7.

16. "Language & Literature: English and American," p. 1752.

17. Patricia Goodfellow, "Book Reviews: Fiction," *Library Journal* 100 (15 September 1975):1651. In a letter from Vincent Cronin (30 June 1984) he writes: "[*Desmonde*], a work of old age, requires, I believe, little space."

18. Robert C. Healey, p. 84.

Chapter Nine

1. Vincent Cronin, "Recollections of a Writer," *Tablet* 235 (21 February 1981):176.

2. Ibid.

3. Ibid.

4. Letter from Vincent Cronin, 30 June 1984.

5. Vincent Cronin, "Recollections of a Writer," p. 175.

6. Ibid., p. 176.

7. Ibid., p. 175.

8. Ibid., p. 176.

Selected Bibliography

PRIMARY SOURCES

1. Fiction

Hatter's Castle. Boston: Little, Brown; London: Gollancz, 1931.
Three Loves. Boston: Little, Brown; London: Gollancz, 1932.
Grand Canary. Boston: Little, Brown, 1933; London: Gollancz, 1934.
The Stars Look Down. Boston: Little, Brown, 1935; London: Gollancz, 1936.
The Citadel. Boston: Little, Brown; London: Gollancz, 1937.
The Keys of the Kingdom. Boston: Little, Brown, 1941; London: Gollancz, 1942.
The Green Years. Boston: Little, Brown, 1944; London: Gollancz, 1945.
Shannon's Way. Boston: Little, Brown; London: Gollancz, 1948.
The Spanish Gardener. Boston: Little, Brown; London: Gollancz, 1950.
Beyond this Place. Boston: Little, Brown; London: Gollancz, 1953.
A Thing of Beauty. Boston: Little, Brown, 1956. Published in England as *Crusader's Tomb.* London: Gollancz, 1956.
The Northern Light. Boston: Little, Brown; London: Gollancz, 1958.
The Judas Tree. Boston: Little, Brown; London: Gollancz, 1961.
A Song of Sixpence. Boston: Little, Brown; London: Heinemann, 1964.
A Pocketful of Rye. Boston: Little, Brown; London: Heinemann, 1969.
Adventures of a Black Bag. London: New English Library, 1969.
Desmonde. Boston: Little, Brown, 1975. Published in England as *The Minstrel Boy.* London: Gollancz, 1975.
Doctor Finlay of Tannochbrae. London: New English Library, 1978.

2. Other Prose

A History of Aneurism. M.D. thesis, 1925.
Report on Dust Inhalation in Haematite Mines. London: His Majesty's Stationery Office, 1926.
Investigations in First-Aid Organization at Collieries in Great Britain. London: His Majesty's Stationery Office, 1927.
Adventures in Two Worlds. New York: McGraw-Hill; London: Gollancz, 1952.

3. Drama

Jupiter Laughs (produced Glasgow and New York, 1940). Boston: Little, Brown, 1940; London: Gollancz, 1941, 1954.

SECONDARY SOURCES

1. Bibliographies

Salwak, Dale. *A. J. Cronin: A Reference Guide.* Boston: G. K. Hall, 1982. First and foremost an annotated listing of the judgments passed on Cronin, the writer and the man, by his English and American readers from 1931 until his passing in 1981. Includes close to 1200 reviews, essays, interviews, bibliographies, and biographical notes as well as an introduction in which the author traces the development of Cronin's literary reputation.

2. Selected Essays and Reviews

Abelard, Peter. "New Novels: *Grand Canary.*" *Times Literary Supplement* (London), 18 May 1933, p. 346. This novel lacks the "intensity" of his two earlier books, but displays the same "powers of graphic narrative."

Bartlett, Arthur. "A. J. Cronin: The Writing Doctor." *Coronet* 35 (March 1954):165–69. Lengthy profile of Cronin the man, the physician, and the writer.

Binsse, H. L. "Fiction." *Commonweal* 34 (1 August 1941):354–55. Contrasts *The Keys of the Kingdom* to works by Graham Greene and Kate O'Brien. While it is a "good story," Cronin's novel is "misleading."

Brégy, Katherine. "New Books." *Catholic World* 160 (January 1945):375. *The Green Years* is for "the mature and sophisticated reader, told with artistry, verisimilitude and the irony of the backward perspective."

Bullett, Gerald. "New Novels." *New Statesman and Nation* 3 (5 March 1932):300. Finds elements of tragedy in *Three Loves.* Comments on Cronin's "imaginative energy and technical assurance."

Caswell, Wilbur Larremore. Review of *The Keys of the Kingdom.* *Churchman* 155 (1 September 1941):21. Recommends that every clergyman read this novel, and hopes that attacks against it will not prejudice anyone.

Cazamian, Louis, and Raymond Las Vergnas. "The Twentieth Century (1914–1963): Chapter I: The Novel and the Short Story." In *A History of English Literature: Book VIII.* New York: Macmillan Company, 1964, p. 1411. As a "prolific storyteller," Cronin delighted many readers with *The Citadel, The Green Years,* and *The Keys of the Kingdom.*

Clarke, Alan Burton. "Fiction." *Bookman* 74 (September 1931):79–80. Discusses elements of the Victorian novel in *Hatter's Castle.* Calls it "a long, solid, meaty book, distinguished for its objective writing and its rich and moving humanity."

Corcoran, Marguerite Page. "New Books." *Catholic World* 167 (August 1948):474–75. Discusses Robert Shannon's perseverance in *Shannon's Way.*

Cort, John C. "Communications." *Commonweal* 34 (29 August 1941):447. Defends *The Keys of the Kingdom* against attacks by other critics.

Cronin, Vincent. "Recollection of a Writer." *Tablet* 235 (21 February 1981):175–76. An appreciation of Cronin written by one of his surviving sons. Includes biographical material and quotes from two messages of sympathy sent to the family.

Dangerfield, George. "Decline and Fall." *Saturday Review of Literature* 7 (18 July 1931):972. Compares *Hatter's Castle* to the classic nineteenth-century novel.

Davenport, Basil. "Chasing Balloons." *Saturday Review of Literature* 8 (2 April 1933):633. Finds similarity between *Three Loves* and Greek tragedy. Calls the novel "another dour, . . . and memorable book."

Davies, Daniel Horton. "Pilgrims, Not Strangers." In his *A Mirror of the Ministry in Modern Novels.* New York: Oxford University Press, 1959, pp. 113–28. Compares and contrasts the portrayal of a Protestant missionary in Maugham's *Rain* and Cronin's depiction in *Grand Canary* and *The Keys of the Kingdom.*

Dukes, Ashley. "The London Scene: Midwinter View." *Theatre Arts* 24 (November 1940):180. *Jupiter Laughs* is both "escapist and history." Feels that this would make a better movie than play.

Fadiman, Clifton. "Books: Inside a Nazi—Dr. Cronin's Saint." *New Yorker* 17 (26 July 1941):46, 49. Except for a few exciting scenes, this novel is tedious. Cronin knows the tricks of the trade, yet this is not the way saints live in the world.

Fitt, Frank. "The Saint As a Best Seller." *Christian Century* 58 (3 September 1941):1081–82. Discusses the characterization and moral values in *The Keys of the Kingdom.*

Frederick, John T. "A. J. Cronin." *College English* 3 (November 1941):121–29. Considers whether or not Cronin may be deemed a great novelist. Discusses in depth the first five novels.

Fytton, Francis. "Dr. Cronin: An Essay in Victoriana." *Catholic World* 183 (August 1956):356–62. Discusses the man behind the novels and his religious thinking since his return to Catholicism. Divides the novels into two groups: those before *The Keys of the Kingdom* and those after.

Greene, Graham. "Fiction." *Spectator* 150 (19 May 1933):728. Criticizes *Grand Canary* as "a perfect example of the Popular Novelist."

Hawthorne, Hazel. "Twice-Told Tale." *New Republic* 68 (16 September 1931):133. Finds similarities between *Hatter's Castle* and selected novels by Thomas Hardy, George Eliot, and Emily Brontë.

Hutchinson, Percy. "*Hatter's Castle*, A Novel in the Great Tradition." *New York Times Book Review*, 19 July 1931, p. 4. Views this novel as the most important English novel in decades, for it marks a return to the nineteenth-century novel.

────── . "The Clash of Capital and Labor." *New York Times Book Review*, 22 September 1935, pp. 1, 23. In *The Stars Look Down* Cronin is "uncannily like Dickens."

Kazin, Alfred. "Dr. Cronin's Novel about the Medical Profession." *New York Times Book Review*, 12 September 1937, p. 6. Comments on Cronin's development since *Hatter's Castle*.

"*The Keys of the Kingdom:* In His Third Best Seller Scotland's Writing Doctor Takes Faith for His Theme." *Life* 11 (24 October 1941):60, 62, 64–66. Biographical essay covering the circumstances under which Cronin wrote *The Keys of the Kingdom*. Includes photographs of him with his family and an essay by Cronin himself entitled "How I Came to Write a Novel of a Priest: For Ten Years His Character Worried Me."

Kunkel, Francis L. "The Priest As Scapegoat in the Modern Catholic Novel." *Ramparts* 1 (January 1963):72. Discusses the archetype of the priest as a Christ-like scapegoat in *The Keys of the Kingdom*.

Lee, Charles. "Fraying Margins of Error." *Saturday Review of Literature* 36 (25 July 1953):14. Compares *Beyond this Place* to the other novels and quotes Cronin about the writing of this novel.

Levin, Martin. "A Reader's Report." *New York Times Book Review*, 18 October 1964, p. 43. *A Song of Sixpence* is a variation of Cronin's earlier novels.

MacAfee, Helen. "The Library of the Quarter: Outstanding Novels." *Yale Review*, n.s. 21 (Autumn 1931):viii, x. *Hatter's Castle* is too logical and too predictable, but based on "physical fact."

McCleary, Dorothy. "Good Reading." *New Republic* 105 (28 July 1941):125. *The Keys of the Kingdom* is "painstakingly documented, and written with narrative frenzy and craftmanship."

McSorley, Joseph. "New Books." *Catholic World* 153 (August

1941):631–32. In *The Keys of the Kingdom* the characters are "pawns, wooden images, caricatures crudely fashioned, or crudely distorted."

Marsh, Fred T. "In the Great English Tradition." *New York Herald-Tribune Books,* 19 July 1931, pp. 3–4. *Hatter's Castle* is a "classic" novel, and yet its concerns are modern.

————. "The Pride of Possessiveness." *New York Herald-Tribune Books,* 3 April 1932, p. 5. Calls *Three Loves* a "more genuine piece of work" than was *Hatter's Castle.* Comments on Cronin's depiction of convent life in the novel.

Mitgang, Herbert. "A. J. Cronin, Author of *Citadel* and *Keys of the Kingdom,* Dies." *New York Times,* 10 January 1981, p. 16. Biographical sketch and brief discussion of Cronin's most popular novels.

Munn, L. S. "An Owner-Editor Meets the Test." *Springfield Republican,* 13 July 1958, p. 5C. Says that *The Northern Light* will disappoint even Cronin's most ardent admirers.

O., P. "Archibald Joseph Cronin." *Catholic Authors: Contemporary Biographical Sketches 1930–1947.* Edited by Matt Hoehn. Newark: St. Mary's Abbey, 1947, pp. 175–76. Biographical background through *The Keys of the Kingdom.*

Pippett, Roger. "Facing the Final Deadline." *New York Times Book Review,* 25 May 1958, p. 4. In Harry Page (*The Northern Light*) Cronin has found "a crusader worthy of his talent and his narrative flair."

————. "Memory of Love." *New York Times Book Review,* 15 October 1961, p. 46. Praises the elements of romance, realism, and moral commentary in *The Judas Tree,* but finds that the characters are contrived.

Prescott, Orville. "Books of the Times." *New York Times,* 27 August 1950, p. 17. Finds in *The Spanish Gardener* some of those qualities that have made Cronin so popular with readers: his personality, sincerity, concern with ethical issues, gifts for storytelling, and knowledge of ordinary people.

————. "Outstanding Novels." *Yale Review* 34 (Winter 1945): 382–83. Finds in *The Green Years* certain qualities that redeem Cronin's shortcomings, including "his intimate knowledge of the troubles of life, his warm sympathy, his identity with almost universal experience."

Proteus [pseud.]. "New Novels." *New Statesman and Nation* 1 (6 June 1931):547. Comments on the presence of an overwhelming sense of fate in *Hatter's Castle*—a theme that controls Cronin.

Quennell, Peter. "New Novels." *New Statesman and Nation* 9 (6 April 1935):490. Comments on the honesty in *The Stars Look Down.*

Raven, Simon. "Maiden Voyage." *Spectator* 200 (5 December 1958):835. A discussion of the characterization and morality in *The Northern Light.*

Ross, Mary. "Life Before the War." *Survey Graphic* 24 (November 1935):557–58. Studies the elements of naturalism in *The Stars Look Down.*

Russell, Richard M. "Cronin's Book Tells Tale of Young Doctor." *Catholic Messenger,* 4 November 1948, p. 11. In *Shannon's Way* the scenes between hero and heroine are "tenderly done," and the ideas are challenging.

Salveson, Christopher. "Et in Somalia Ego." *New Statesman* 68 (31 July 1964):155. Discusses the oversimplified characters and the lack of continuity.

Salwak, Dale. "A. J. Cronin." In *Critical Survey of Long Fiction,* edited by Frank A. Magill, 1:648–62. New Jersey: Salem Press, 1983. Brief analysis of *Hatter's Castle, The Stars Look Down, The Citadel, The Keys of the Kingdom,* and *The Green Years.* Includes biographical background and consideration of other literary forms by Cronin.

Shucard, Alan R. "Cronin, A(rchibald) J(oseph)." In *Contemporary Novelists.* Edited by James Vinson. 2d ed. London: St. James' Press; New York: St. Martin's Press, 1975, pp. 327–29. Lists Cronin's publications through 1975 and traces his reputation and career.

Strong, L. A. G. "Fiction." *Spectator* 148 (27 February 1932):298. *Three Loves* has "great power and distinction," but it is "long-winded." Lucy Moore's character lacks strength or power.

————. "Fiction: the Rough and the Smooth." *Spectator* 146 (30 May 1931):870, 872. Discusses *Hatter's Castle* as a major achievement in fiction.

Uden, Grant. "The Bookman Gallery: A. J. Cronin." *Bookman* 76 (March 1933):494. A detailed analysis of Cronin's first three novels. Pays attention to characterization, romantic plots, and vision. Includes a commentary on *Kaleidoscope in K.*

Ulrich, Mabel S., M.D. "Doctor's Dilemma." *Saturday Review* (London), 16 (11 September 1937):5–6. Analyzes the themes in *The Citadel* and compares the novel to Cronin's earlier works.

Van Doren, Dorothy. "Death, Destruction, and Power." *Nation* 133 (29 July 1931):113–14. Of *Hatter's Castle,* she says: "Not since *Wuthering Heights* have we had a horror story that so completely satisfies all the requirements of the genre."

Walpole, Hugh. "Books Abroad: London Letter, June." *New York*

Herald-Tribune Books, 28 June 1932, p. 9. Sees in *Hatter's Castle* a step in the return of "the objective novel to English fiction." Compares Cronin to Thomas Hardy.

Weidman, Jerome. "Books: Dr. Cronin's New Novel Full of 'Incredible Hokum.' " *PM's Weekly,* 20 July 1941, p. 44. Calls *The Keys of the Kingdom* "a classic of corn, bad taste, insufferable writing and public hoodwinking." Prompted an outcry by Cronin's defenders.

Williams, Orlo. "Recent Fiction Chronicle." *Criterion* 11 (October 1931):88–89. *Hatter's Castle* is a first novel of "undoubted merit," but questions the merits in calling Cronin "a new star of great brilliance."

Williams, William Carlos. "Books and the Arts: A Good Doctor's Story." *Nation* 145 (11 September 1937):268. *The Citadel* is not a "great novel" in the sense that Norman Douglas or Ford Madox Ford would speak of a great novel, but it is a "good novel."

Wyatt, Euphenia Van Rensselaer. "The Drama: *Jupiter Laughs."* *Catholic World* 152 (October 1940):89. Essay on the writing, characterization, plotting, and psychology of *Jupiter Laughs.*

Index